1990

Decade of Novels

Fiction of the 1970s:
Form and Challenge

Decade of Novels

Fiction of the 1970s:
Form and Challenge

Charles Berryman

The Whitston Publishing Company
Troy, New York
1990

Contents

Introduction

Once upon a time fiction was thought to be a mirror held up to nature. Or was it life that imitated art? Now that fiction and reality are both considered problematic, the question itself has been deconstructed. Fiction has become metafiction, fabulation, surfiction, the new novel, anti-fiction, and postmodern signs. Reality has fallen into the linguistic gap between the signifier and the signified. Where does that leave the contemporary novel?

While critics in the 1970s were engaged like armies clashing by night, the ten authors in this study were creating a remarkable decade of novels. The voices from current events were often anticipated in the pages of fiction. The final scenes of Watergate—"I am not a crook"— did not appear on the stage of history until more than two years after Philip Roth had dramatized the antic behavior of Trick E. Dixon in *Our Gang*. The experience of Patricia Hearst—"I am a soldier in the people's army"—only became news three years after John Updike had created a similar character in *Rabbit Redux*. The mass suicide in Jonestown—"It is beautiful to die"— took place four years after Toni Morrison had dramatized National Suicide Day in *Sula*.

If current events and contemporary novels are created by imitation in either direction, then most definitions of realism merely beg the question, and the mixture of life and art cannot be undone. Norman Mailer implies as much when he uses "History as a Novel/ The Novel as History" for the subtitle of *The Armies of the Night*. Given this premise, what is the proper role for literary criticism? Despite all of the recent interest in self-reflexive fiction, the problem cannot be solved by shifting the critical focus exclusively to the strategies of art. No matter how self-conscious the novel becomes, it cannot exist solely as a reflection of itself, nor as a parody of its own artistic conventions. The blank pages in *Tristram Shandy* are the *ne plus ultra* of that strategy. Nor does it help for critics to imitate the forms of fiction—reflexive, disconnected, inconclusive—that are supposedly being analyzed. Small wonder that Toni Morrison complains that criticism is "following postmodern fiction into self-consciousness."

The title of this book implies an intersection of history and fiction. The ten chapters focus in turn on one novel published each year from *Mr. Sammler's Planet* in 1970 to the comic satire of Joseph Heller's *Good as Gold* in 1979. The ten authors chosen to represent the decade are diverse, but all have made a significant contribution towards defining the form and challenge of contemporary fiction.

The first chapter is a departure from the critical position that identifies the author of *Mr. Sammler's Planet* with the opinions and attitudes of the title character. Instead, the novel is viewed as a contemporary retelling of *King Lear*. The madness that Mr. Sammler sees as a threat to his world is the same force of anger and pride that Shakespeare reveals on his stage of fools. The metaphor of life as a drama is where history and fiction come together. If the natural tempest in *King Lear* is a symbol of the rage and confusion in Lear's mind, the increasing violence in *Mr. Sammler's Planet* is a reflection of the anxiety and stubbornness of Bellow's one-eyed prophet.

The next chapter on John Updike's *Rabbit Redux* (1971) is a study of the way current events—Apollo 11 and Vietnam—are used to form an illusion of history. The controlling images of the fiction come from the TV coverage of space exploration and military failure. The hero of the novel loses both job and home after the images of space and war begin to invade his life in suburban America. Although he starts as a passive witness to contemporary violence, the protagonist soon finds himself on the stage where betrayal and death are possible.

The chapter on Margaret Atwood's *Surfacing* (1972) is a genre study of the forms of self-discovery in her narrative. The heroine travels into the natural landscape of her childhood in order to find a missing parent, the significance of her own history, and the freedom necessary for a fresh beginning. Her journey is not only a contemporary version of a descent into the underworld, it is also a re-enactment of the patterns typical of comedy and romance. The oldest patterns of myth and drama are thus reflected in recent fiction.

The next chapter is an exploration of self-parody in a contemporary novel. Kurt Vonnegut's *Breakfast of Champions* (1973) demonstrates the comedy of a novelist who appears as a character in his own fiction. Vonnegut is trying to sabotage the conventional author/

audience relationship in order to carry forward a game of self-mockery and a comic satire. The result is a novel which reads like a möbius strip—the inside and outside of the twisted loop continuously interchange.

The chapter on Toni Morrison's *Sula* (1974) is a study of what happens when an individual character is set up against a background of community disapproval. The narrative method, not to mention the tone and imagery of the novel, depends upon Morrison's access to the folklore, history, and conversation of a threatened community. The flashbacks in the novel tell the history of three generations, and draw the reader into the story of a disappearing neighborhood, a drama of multiple betrayal, and the tragic dilemma of a character who is undone by her own free spirit.

The next chapter explores the collage of fiction and history in E. L. Doctorow's *Ragtime* (1975). The narrator is a minor character in the novel who collects the fragments of the past and assembles them with an inexplicable knowledge of the future. The novel includes a gallery of portraits—Henry Ford, Sigmund Freud, J. P. Morgan, Booker T. Washington, Evelyn Nesbit, Emma Goldman, and Harry Houdini—all from a decade before the first World War, but the collage of urban terror, political confusion, and feminist concern still reflects the experience of the 1970s.

The chapter on John Hawkes's *Travesty* (1976) looks at a contemporary example of gothic literature. The novel is a dramatic monologue spoken by a character who is driving a car at high speed in the direction of a stone wall. Suicide and murder are his aims, but until the crash he speaks to his captive passengers in a confidential, mysterious, and rather disturbing manner. The reader becomes an unwilling passenger in the car headed for disaster. It is impossible to know what to accept as real in a monologue that may all be the fantasy of a deranged narrator.

The next chapter on Philip Roth's *The Professor of Desire* (1977) examines a narrator who explains his own predicament in terms of previous fiction. Roth's victim finds literary precedents in the stories of Chekhov and Kafka. The novel follows the education, literary and sexual, of a narrator who is destined to become the object of his own wildest desires. The future of the narrator is an unexpected and fantastic imitation of his favorite literature.

The final chapters on Gore Vidal's *Kalki* (1978) and Joseph

Heller's *Good as Gold* (1979) are explorations of satire. Vidal mocks the extravagance of religious superstition in the 1970s, and Heller makes fun of politics, social climbing, and the career of Henry Kissinger. In both novels current events are presented in caricature, and the world is seen as a stage of fools and charlatans.

"There never was a time," says Leslie Fiedler, "when more different kinds of fiction were being written." No consensus exists about the design or definition of the contemporary novel. The critical methods in this book include a study of genre, metaphor, narrative technique, self-parody, collage, satire, etc. All ten authors have found their separate voices, explored their particular visions, and created works of fiction that have their own coherence. It is the aim of this book to meet each author on his or her own territory, and thus to explore from year to year the literature of the 1970s.

1970

Saul Bellow
Mr. Sammler's Planet

At the beginning of the decade no living American novelist enjoyed a better critical reputation than Saul Bellow. Others may have earned more from paperback and film rights, but no one commanded more attention from prize committees and academic critics. The question about the Nobel Prize was not "if" but "when." After a remarkable success with *Herzog* in the mid 1960s Bellow was prepared to start the new decade with the publication of *Mr. Sammler's Planet*. Some of his admirers, however, had expectations for the new novel which could hardly be fulfilled. If the character of Herzog could write letters to everyone from Socrates to God, it was hoped that the next novel by his creator would be an important philosophical statement. Critics were ready for Bellow to take a "stand against the cultural nihilism of the twentieth century."[1] The novelist cannot be held responsible for the confusion of literature and philosophy inherent in such hopes, but his fiction has often been praised by those looking for a qualified affirmation of life in the pages of literature. When a critic tells us that "Bellow affirms the possibilities of meaningful individual life," should we rejoice in a victory for literature, or confess that Matthew Arnold was right a century ago when he predicted that "most of what now passes with us for religion and philosophy will be replaced by poetry?"

The impossible hopes about the nature and purpose of literature have been encouraged by a series of critical books. At the head of the list is Ihab Hassan's *Radical Innocence: Studies in the Contemporary American Novel* (1961). "The function of American fiction," declares Hassan, "is to mediate between the hero's outrageous dream and the sadness of human mortality."[2] Never mind the number of questions hiding in such an assertion—what is meant by "function," "dream," etc. As soon as the novel is viewed as a "dialectical form" which "mediates between self and world," the critic is free to talk about "man's quenchless desire to affirm . . . man's alienation . . . the ontological problem of man's being . . . the stark encounter with nothingness," etc.[3] Philosophical and religious statements thus grow like weeds, innocently rooted, in the field of literary criticism. Each hero in Bellow's fiction is regarded by Hassan as a test case for "man" and each plot becomes an "existential situation."

A similar mixture of literary criticism and wishful thinking appears a few years later in Marcus Klein's *After Alienation: American Novels in Mid-Century* (1964). "The dialogue between alienation and accommodation," Klein declares of Bellow's work, "is what the novels first of all are about."[4] Who can reply to a critical voice asserting a vision of first things? "The social progress of the sensible hero of our time," Klein argues, "has been from a position of alienation toward accommodation." What evidence could support this critical jargon? Klein points to a *Partisan Review* symposium held in 1952 as proof of the turning point—a firm indication that "most writers no longer accept alienation as the artist's fate in America." How many artists ever did? Saul Bellow does have close ties with the *Partisan Review*, and it may even be true that *The Adventures of Augie March* (1953) has a more accommodating hero than either *Dangling Man* (1944) or *The Victim* (1947), but what is achieved by attempting to measure literary or social history with such cant terms?

Semi-religious and philosophical statements continue to masquerade as literary criticism the next year in Jonathan Baumbach's *The Landscape of Nightmare* (1965). "Our recent novels," claims Baumbach, "are almost paradigms of the existential possibilities (and impossibilities) of sainthood."[5] He is a firm believer in the view of Hassan that a novel should be a "test case of our moral and aesthetic life." Baumbach argues that all of Bellow's novels "deal with the sufferer, the seismographic recorder of world guilt who, confronted by a guilt-distorted correlative of himself, seeks within the bounds of his own hell the means to his heaven."[6] Given the theological drift of the language, it is hardly surprising that Baumbach analyses each novel as a spiritual passage from guilt to redemption. The happy conclusion, no doubt, will please all of the readers eager to find in Bellow's work an affirmation of "the possibility of meaningful existence." What can the word "heaven" possibly mean in Baumbach's sentence? How does Augie March achieve a form of sainthood? Or are the religious terms in Baumbach's criticism rather desperate and empty metaphors?

Until the mid '60s published critical work on Bellow was confined to essays, reviews, and chapters in books like those discussed above. Then the confusion of literary criticism and moral philosophy took a quantum leap into monographs on Saul Bellow. One of the best, John Clayton's *Saul Bellow: In Defense of Man* (1968), is still typical of the dialogue between "hero" and "world" stressed by Hassan. "In so much of Bellow's fiction," writes Clayton, "there is an alienated hero struggling to redeem his own life—and, by extension, the common life."[7] The word "alienated" is still in fashion, the assumed goal of the fictional hero is the familiar "redemption," and his success will somehow provide a paradigm for "the common life." The very title of the book suggests its moral optimism. Clayton is very good at exploring some of the contradictions inherent in his critical terms, but he never suggests that a different vocabulary might be preferable. He is also quite good when it comes to a psychological analysis of specific characters, but the analysis is still subordinated to the doubtful metaphysics of alienation and redemption.

Clayton's work on the novels of Saul Bellow began with a doctoral dissertation at Indiana University. More than forty dissertations have now been completed on the fiction of Bellow—a clear indication of the need to provide material for the critical mill and the desire to praise a writer who "stands as a spokesman for our culture." The title of the first doctoral thesis ever written on Bellow's fiction— "What's the Best Way to Live: A Study of the Novels of Saul Bellow"— suggests the bias of the genre.[8] Matthew Arnold's prediction that literature would become a guide to moral conduct is doing especially well in graduate schools.

The litany of semi-religious statements continues in the criticism of the 1970s. "The direction of all Bellow's work," claims Tony Tanner, "is moving towards a lonely encounter with the ultimate mysteries."[9] Is this a statement about Bellow's fiction, or a reminder that life is fatal? Herzog and Sammler, of course, are fictional characters very much concerned with death. So are Antigone and Hamlet. "What drives Herzog on," Tanner would have us believe, "is the will to deny the universal truth of the law of entropy."[10] Such an abstract statement might appeal to Moses Herzog, but it hardly illuminates the novel.

As soon as *Mr. Sammler's Planet* appeared its ironic style was hailed as a means to "reconcile the paradoxical nature of religious faith."[11] Another critic described the title character as a "way into blessedness and felicity."[12] Perhaps the worst that can be said about Bellow is that he occasionally appears to think like his critics and admirers. Maybe his books are designed for an audience in need of a secular faith with the right degree of intellectual concern and moral affirmation. Leslie Fiedler at least thinks that Bellow is a sellout to middle-class optimism.[13] If this is true, then Bellow and his audience deserve one another. It is more likely, however, that Fiedler is incorrect, and that Bellow's art is better served by separating him from both the fictional heroes of his novels and the religious desires of his readers. While the bewildered Herzog is thinking about writing a number of different books, it is Saul Bellow who creates the novel. The nature of his art, not the metaphysical clouds of his protagonist, should be the subject of literary criticism.

Nothing is more prevalent in the growing volume of critical writing on Bellow than a shift of attention from the work of art to the ideas of the author. Each of his novels from *Dangling Man* to *The Dean's December* tends to focus on the mind of one individual, and therefore each has been read as a progressive stage in the autobiography of the novelist. Such criticism is natural enough, and no doubt contains some truth, but it scarcely does justice to the quality of fiction. *Mr. Sammler's Planet* has been widely misinterpreted as an account of Bellow's own bitter view of the modern world. While the beat of the drums was mounting for the Nobel Prize, who could separate the novel from the growing celebrity of its author? The confusion of author and title character leads unwary readers to accept the views of Sammler without considering his eccentricity and possible madness.

Although the mind of Mr. Sammler is the focal point of Bellow's novel, the events of the book are not narrated in the first person. Instead, the voice of the author presents the thoughts and actions of the protagonist. Thus we have a chance to view Sammler from the outside, and the description often verges on caricature—"He had the face of a British Museum reader."[14] His one good eye peers "through the overhanging hairs of the brow as in some breeds of dog" (4). Such ironic descriptions scarcely give him stature as a seer or prophet.

Bellow's critical distance from his fictional character was not well perceived when the novel first appeared. Several reviewers accused Bellow of sharing the reactionary and bitter views of Mr. Sammler. Alfred Kazin, his friendship with the author notwithstanding, wrote that Sammler is "openly Bellow's mind now."[15] Surely any attempt to identify the novelist with his main character should be qualified by the degree of caricature in Sammler's portrait. It is a comic mistake to confuse Saul Bellow with his tall, one-eyed, impoverished septuagenarian.

Biographical speculation becomes a special nuisance when the man behind the mask is already overexposed to the public. Although he deplores the news of "publicity intellectuals," Bellow's reputation naturally keeps him in the spotlight. Shortly after the publication of the novel Bellow contributed an essay to *Modern Occasions*.[16] The opinions in the essay are close enough to Mr. Sammler's to cause further suspicion about the identity of author and character. Worse yet, Bellow let slip in an interview for *Life* that "I'm baring myself nakedly" in *Mr. Sammler's Planet*.[17] After such a confession, the art needs to be rescued from the artist. It would be strange indeed if Bellow and Sammler did not have some similarities of thought and expression. Critical distance, however, is always a matter of degree, and it is the crucial difference between reading the novel as a dramatic work of art and reducing it to biographical statements.

The confusion of author and character often reinforces the popular desire to promote both as important voices of philosophy and culture. Much of the critical attention therefore has been spent on Bellow's supposed indictment of contemporary America. The bitter views of Sammler are not only attributed to Bellow himself, they are also treated as profound cultural and philosophical statements. Thus it is claimed that *Mr. Sammler's Planet* is a "book of lamentations about the difficulties of being a humanist in this world."[18] In the eighth decade of his life Sammler does possess some unusual credentials as a Jeremiah: he can survey American character from the shifting vantage points of his European past, and he can study the behavior of the late 1960s with a conscience that is older than the century. Is it possible, however, to write a jeremiad for a modern audience more accustomed to hear: "I am no prophet—and here's no great matter?" How would a "book of lamentations" for the end of the twentieth century engage a skeptical audience? Mr. Sammler in fact is a most unreliable seer and prophet. His thoughts and actions are dramatized by Bellow with an ironic eye to the pretensions and madness of a self-appointed doomsayer.

Saul Bellow was writing the novel when the first American astronauts were landing on the moon. The early drafts show that "Future of the Moon" was the intended title, but with second thoughts Bellow decided to use that title for the odd manuscript of a secondary character. "Future of the Moon" thus became a book within a book, and it stands as an ironic mirror in Bellow's novel.[19] The supposed author of "Future of the Moon" is a comic Indian scientist, Govinda Lal, who believes that colonies ought to be immediately established on the moon. The long discussion between Mr. Sammler and Dr. Lal has been praised as an "earnest airing of views on matters of great import," and Bellow's novel has accordingly been accepted as a "distinguished novel of ideas."[20] Nonsense. Such uncritical praise tends to miss the irony of the novel, and to ignore the possibility that Bellow's main character may be touched with lunacy.

Mr. Sammler's Planet is Bellow's first novel with a protagonist who is a very old man, and for the first time Bellow gives dramatic substance to the relationship of fathers and their grown children. The most appropriate model for Sammler is neither Teresias nor Jeremiah, it is King Lear. Sammler is approaching four score years, and he tragically misjudges both his daughter and his son-in-law. Also in the novel is another old man, Elya Gruner, with two grown children who are accused of mad schemes and ingratitude. The fathers who cannot accept their own children must learn like Lear and Gloucester what it means to be mad and blind. The children who feel rejected by their proud and intolerant parents must suffer a form of exile reminiscent of Cordelia and Edgar.

Bellow's novel has been accused of having no plot, but it actually follows rather closely the dramatic outline of Shakespeare's play. At the beginning Sammler is a very self-righteous intemperate, and proud old man. He is described as "explosive" and "violent." Sammler no longer lives with his only daughter because her life style often sent him into "fits of rage." Shula merely wants to please her father, but he blames her for his "series of attacks," and has decided to live with another relative. Although the daughter is repeatedly criticized, she still tries to bring help to her father. Shula and Cordelia have some obvious differences, but their roles are essentially the same—it is their father's business they go about. Separated from his well-intentioned daughter, Sammler naturally feels exposed to a hostile world. Some of the madness he sees, however, is a reflection of the confusion in his own mind. Nightmares of suffering, violence, and death all rage together in his head. His condition is no less painful because he happens to be more sinned against than sinning. Lear's mad trial of his daughters is matched by Sammler's penchant for judging all of his relatives. He too sees the world as a "great stage of fools," and feels compelled to preach to his blind companions. For three days in the novel Sammler is bound upon a wheel of fire, but in the end he is reconciled with Shula, and his last words to her are: "You're a good daughter. The best of any. No better daughter."

The subplot of Elya Gruner and his two children is parallel in several ways to the story of Gloucester. Gruner is introduced like his Shakespearean counterpart as a rather sympathetic and gregarious man who is essentially blind to the identities of his children. He thinks that his son Wallace is an ungrateful madcap who should be prevented from his wild schemes, but it may be that Wallace is forced by his father's rejection to imitate the behavior of Tom o' Bedlam. Gruner thinks that his daughter Angela is no better than a nymphomaniac, but it may be that Angela's sexual license is merely her response to her father's secret life as an abortionist for the Mafia. Gruner and Gloucester are both ambiguous characters: amiable yet shadowed with unacknowledged crime, sympathetic yet incapable of seeing their own culpability, and in each case their transgressions have to do with sexual misconduct. There is, however, no scene of reconciliation for Gruner in the novel. He dies in bitterness, not smilingly, and he dies alone, despite the fact that his daughter is in the waiting room and his son in his own predictable way is trying to make his presence felt.

The subject of madness in *Mr. Sammler's Planet* is as significant and complex as it is in Shakespeare's play. At the beginning Sammler is subject to "fits of rage" caused by "damage to his nervous system," yet his unsympathetic treatment of Shula does not appear wholly unreasonable. Bellow is primarily showing us things from Sammler's point of view, and thus we are apt to be taken in by his curious judgment. When he begins to think of others as mad—dismissing his daughter as "obviously a nut"—we may wonder about Sammler's judgment, but we cannot see at once that he is making the same kind of mistake as Lear. Although several hints of eccentricity are included in the initial description of Sammler, it is only when he dwells himself on the subject of madness that we begin to wonder if the many pressures on his mind will prove too great a burden. Lear pleads with the gods: "O, let me not be mad, not mad, sweet heaven!" and Sammler asks if it is possible to survive the "crazy fervor . . . the strange erotic persuasions . . . the psychic atmosphere . . . the madness overwhelming the Western world." Nothing is more typical of Sammler than to imagine some ultimate disintegration. "A whole nation," he tells himself, "is seeking the blameless state of madness."

If it is true that Lear "hath ever but slenderly known himself," the same liability is shared by Sammler. Only a few pages into the novel Bellow reports that Sammler "didn't in fact appear to know his age, or at what point of life he stood" (6). Perhaps that statement should be kept in mind by the critics who praise Sammler's "wise comments on the lunacy of our age." The limited self-knowledge of both characters reduces their chances of retaining sanity.

The pressure on Lear's mind increases when he is exposed to feel what wretches feel in the pitiless storm. Sammler also is battered by mental and physical forces. Haunted by the image of himself as "an old Jew whom they had hacked at, shot at, but missed killing somehow," he is doomed to relive the trauma of the mass grave, the murder in the Polish forest, and the hiding in the tomb. Sammler witnesses the twentieth century as a repetitive stage of madness and destruction. Bellow's hero might well agree with Joyce's famous words—"History is the nightmare from which I am trying to awaken"—because he has escaped from more than one tomb only to find that life remains a confrontation with death. Even in New York City violence and death appear to hunt him down. Intimidated by a black pickpocket, insulted by angry students, and troubled by a dying relative, the blows at the sanity of Sammler are relentless.

There is a moment in Shakespeare's play when Lear's prayer— "O, let me not be mad"—proves unsuccessful. His mad speeches begin on the night of the storm when he meets Edgar posing as Tom o' Bedlam. Is there a similar transformation in Bellow's novel? Sammler makes a visit one night to the Gruner estate in the company of the madcap Wallace who talks incessantly of the very things that are most disturbing to the old man—the attack of the pickpocket, the murder of a kid by a black gang, and the sudden chance of drowning. This is followed by Sammler's strange interview with Govinda Lal in the temporary sanctuary of Gruner's house. Should we accept their conversation as a perfectly sane discussion about the "Future of the Moon?" Although it has been suggested that "Bellow regards their philosophical exchange as the ideological center of the novel,"[21] it makes more sense to accept the lunar conversation as the moving dialogue of mad Lear and blind Gloucester. "I will preach to thee," says Lear, "mark" (IV, vi, 182). "Oh, but please continue," says Dr. Lal, "we are most attentive" (227).

Sammler of course does continue at great length and with much "matter and impertinancy mixed." He talks passionately about the "awful volume of cumulative consciousness" and condemns his species for its "hereditary deformity." He claims "that most forms of personal existence seem to be discredited, and that there is a peculiar longing for nonbeing" (235). His comments are reminiscent of Lear's indictment of the whole species in the mad trial scene and of his earlier plea to: "Strike flat the thick rotundity o' the' world/Crack Nature's molds, all germains spill at once,/That makes ingrateful man" (III, ii, 7-9). To accept the views of Sammler as "indispensable guides to the perplexities of the times" indicates a comic lapse in perspective.[22] It means identifying with the obsequious Govinda Lal who says "Oh, but please continue." The dialogue of Sammler and Lal is not the "ideological center of the novel," it is an inspired scene of lunacy when the protagonist and his blind audience "Now to the Moon in wavering Morrice move."[23] The moon not only exerts a strange pull on the minds of the two men, it also controls the tides of the planet, and the scene ends comically with an unexpected flood. The philosophical dialogue is suddenly interrupted when the participants discover that their feet are getting wet.

At the center of Sammler's conversation with Govinda Lal is the story of Rumkowski—"the mad Jewish King of Lodz" (230). At the height of the Nazi terror in Poland an old man, "a distasteful fun-figure in the Jewish community," is crowned by the Nazis as a ghetto king. While the children are being killed, and the dead are left in the street for the corpse wagon, Rumkowski is entertained with "pageants and plays organized in his honor." Sammler is fascinated by the memory of the "mad Jewish King presiding over the death of half a million people," but what interests him the most is "the theatricality of the Rumkowski episode." He knows how it pleased the Germans to degrade the Jews with a mock king, but he objects even more to the desperate "theater of the soul." History for Lear and Sammler has become a "great stage of fools."

The madness of Lear is also the purgation of his anger, self-righteousness, and pride. It is the necessary prelude to the reconciliation with his loving daughter. On the final day of the novel Sammler awakens to find that he is alone with Shula. Although he still feels a bit irritable, and would rather be at the bedside of his dying nephew, Sammler for the first time appears to take some interest in his daughter's affection. They sit together on the lawn "penetrated by new growth" and he talks to her about love. "I feel much better," she says, "when you take an interest in me" (265). When he carelessly refers to Wallace as a "lunatic," she asks him why he uses such a word. Bellow then gives us the following account of the old man's thoughts:

> To a lunatic, how would you define a lunatic? And was he himself a perfect example of sanity? He was certainly not. They were his people—he was their Sammler. They shared the same fundamentals. (266)

His self-knowledge is now equal to Lear's admission—"I fear I am not in my perfect mind." Such words and thoughts are the indication of sanity regained. Lear can now recognize his daughter—"I think this lady/To be my child Cordelia"—and Sammler will soon say "You're a good daughter. The best of any."

The second father in the novel dies without any reconciliation with his children. The final evening of his life he says to Sammler: "Let's make it fathers only. I don't want to see children tonight" (177). Elya Gruner is bitterly disappointed in his children: "My daughter is a dirty cunt... And my son, a high-IQ moron." (And this is the father praised by Sammler for his "feeling, outgoingness, expressiveness, kindness, heart"!) Sammler has as much difficulty in recognizing the faults of another father as he does in acknowledging his own faults. In fact, Gruner may be largely responsible for the erratic behavior of his children. Instead of taking a lively interest in the activities of his son, Gruner prefers to discuss the genealogy of dead relatives in Poland. He apparently doesn't recognize that his son's unusual behavior may be nothing more than a desperate attempt to gain a father's attention. Even crash-landing a plane on the day of his father's death may only be Wallace's way of proving that he identifies with the fate of his father. Elya Gruner is also blind to his own responsibility for the behavior of his daughter. While he upholsters his furniture with the money paid by the mafia for illegal abortions, he blames his daughter for her sexual promiscuity.

Unable to talk with her own father, Angela ironically tries to discuss her life with Sammler. He merely listens with impatience, and finally condemns her with the same intolerance characteristic of Gruner. Neither old man can understand that Angela's role as a liberated woman is more than careless and degenerate. Sammler thinks that "strange erotic persuasions" are "overwhelming the Western world" and that Angela's behavior is merely a symptom of "the sexual madness." He cannot see that Angela is responding to her father with his "Mafioso swagger." Sammler's final lecture to Angela about Sodom and Gomorah is irrelevant. "What do *you* know about it?" Angela bitterly replies. Her words echo the taunt of the angry student earlier in the novel: "Why do you listen to this effete old shit? What has he got to tell you? His balls are dry. He's dead. He can't come." Although this "sex-excrement-militancy" is accepted by Sammler as simple evidence of the growing madness of the younger generation, impotence is a metaphor in the novel for the inability of both fathers to accept their own children. Unable to acknowledge their own role as parents, both Sammler and Gruner are disturbed by thoughts of sexual conduct. Sammler is even hunted down by the black pickpocket who then exhibits his penis—"Sammler was required to gaze at this organ. No compulsion would have been necessary. He would in any case have looked" (49). Sammler's fascination is a measure of the sexual fears and desires that surface in his mind as a vision of "the sexual ways of the seraglio and of the Congo bush adopted by the emancipated masses of New York" (32). Sammler's indictment of the sexual conduct of his species is reminiscent of Lear's— "Down from the waist they are Centaurs"—and in either case we see the tragic spectacle of a father who rails against the very power of generation. The tirades of Lear and Sammler are a poor substitute for acknowledging their own flesh and blood in their living daughters.

No audience of Shakespeare's play is likely to accept Lear's mad judgment about the total corruption of the human race, and no reader of Bellow's novel should be fully taken in by the scathing pronouncements of Mr. Sammler. Nevertheless, it is clear from several reviews and essays that many readers have been all too willing to accept the thoughts of Sammler as "indispensable guides to the perplexities of the times." Either the character of Sammler has been accepted as a figure of wisdom—the seer Tiresias—or he has been seen as a reactionary foe of contemporary society—the prophet Jeremiah. Both readings stem from the error of claiming that "the private drama of *Mr. Sammler's Planet* exists only as a vehicle for sounding public proclamations and moral mandates, for getting things off Bellow's chest."[24] Such is the confusion of life and art that was briefly traced at the beginning of this chapter.

Lear is seldom interpreted as a spokesman for Shakespeare or as a cogent guide to his contemporary world. Nor should Sammler be pressed into the service of either role. Instead, we might watch as Lear and Sammler commit their tragic errors, suffer the madness of spirits that are burdened beyond coherence, and still emerge at the end with wiser hearts. "I know when one is dead and when one lives," says Lear in his final grief over the body of Cordelia. Bellow ends his novel with the words of Sammler next to the corpse of his nephew: "For that is the truth of it—that we all know, God, that we know, that we know, we know, we know" (313).

The death of Cordelia evokes stunned comments from Kent—"Is this the promised end?" and Edgar—"Or image of that horror?" Sammler himself often thinks about "the collapse of civilization . . . the end of the world" (304); he wonders if "we are about to conclude our earth business" (148); and Dr. Lal is eager to colonize the moon while there is still time. Sammler, however, is finally convinced that the earth is the right place to "affirm the human bond." Despite his vision of "the suicidal impulses of civilization," it is clear that Sammler is a natural survivor. The only great flood in the novel ironically occurs indoors. Sammler is neither Tiresias surveying the wasteland of "fear in a handful of dust," nor Jeremiah lamenting the "empty cisterns and exhausted wells." Nor does Bellow's version of *King Lear* reach a full tragic conclusion—Sammler after all is still alive—which is appropriate enough for a novel whose protagonist is eccentric, touched with lunacy, endearing, and indestructible.

Notes

[1] John Clayton, *Saul Bellow, In Defense of Man* (Bloomington: Indiana University Press, 1968), p. 4.

[2] Ihab Hassan, *Radical Innocence: Studies in the Contemporary American Novel* (Princeton University Press, 1961), p. 329.

[3] *Ibid.*, pp. 6-19.

[4] Marcus Klein, *After Alienation, American Novels in Mid-Century* (Cleveland: World Publishing, 1964), p. 34.

[5] Jonathan Baumbach, *The Landscape of Nightmare* (New York: University Press, 1965), p. 3.

[6] *Ibid.*, p. 52.

[7] John Clayton, *Saul Bellow, In Defense of Man*, p. 6.

[8] Bessie Michael, "What's the Best Way to Live: A Study of the Novels of Saul Bellow" (Lehigh University, 1960, DA 30, 5451A-2A).

[9] Tony Tanner, *City of Words, American Fiction 1950-1970* (New York: Harper & Row, 1971), p. 308.

[10] *Ibid.*, p. 302.

[11] James Neil Harris, "One Critical Approach to *Mr. Sammler's Planet*," *Twentieth Century Literature*, 18 (October, 1972), 235-270.

[12] Nathan Scott, "Bellow's Vision of the 'Axial Lines'," *Three American Moralists* (Bloomington: Indiana University Press, 1973), pp. 99-150.

[13] Leslie Fiedler, remarks during a symposium "On the Novel Today," YMHA, New York City, March 28, 1965.

[14] *Mr. Sammler's Planet* (New York: Viking Press, 1970), p. 6. Subsequent references to this edition are cited parenthetically.

[15] Alfred Kazin, *Bright Book of Life—American Novelists and Storytellers from Hemingway to Mailer* (Boston: Little, Brown, 1973), p. 136.

[16] Saul Bellow, "Culture Now: Some Animadversions, Some Laughs," *Modern Occasions*, 1 (Winter, 1971), 162-178.

[17] Jane Howard, "Mr. Bellow Considers His Planet," *Life*, 68 (April 3, 1970), 59.

[18] Sarah Cohen, *Saul Bellow's Enigmatic Laughter* (Chicago: University of Illinois Press, 1974), p. 223. Also see Jennifer Bailey, "A Qualified Affirmation of Saul Bellow's Recent Work," *Journal of American Studies*, 7 (April, 1973), 67-76, and D. P. M. Salter, "Optimism and Reaction in Saul Bellow's Recent Work," *Critical Quarterly*, 14 (Spring, 1972), 57-66.

[19] The manuscripts, typescripts, and galley proofs of *Mr. Sammler's Planet* are among the Bellow papers held in the Regenstein Library of the University of Chicago.

[20] Sarah Cohen, *Saul Bellow's Enigmatic Laughter*, p. 199.
[21] *Ibid.*, p. 201.
[22] *Ibid.*, p. 193.
[23] Milton, *Comus*, quoted by Mr. Sammler, p. 97.
[24] Beverly Gross, "Dark Side of the Moon," *Nation*, 210 (February 9, 1970), 155.

1971

John Updike
Rabbit Redux

Is there life for an artist after his face has appeared on the cover of *Time*? John Updike achieved this notoriety in 1968 with the popular success of *Couples*. The rituals of celebrity have often been a risk for American writers. Updike knows what may happen if an author is distracted by success—"a well-intentioned garrulity replaces the specific witness that has been his to give."[1] *Rabbit Redux* is Updike's first novel after the apotheosis of *Time*. Does it give a clear perception of a specific moment in American history—the news of Vietnam and Apollo 11 during the summer and fall of 1969—or does it mix current events with a "well-intentioned garrulity?" The novel has been celebrated as "a paradigm of contemporary American history," and dismissed as "jarring and offensive to both mind and taste."[2] It has been acclaimed as "the best American novel of 1971," and attacked for its "breathtaking ineptitude." Even when the typical exaggeration of reviewers is discounted, the disagreement is extraordinary. Perhaps the loudest complaints are due to the rage of Caliban recognizing his own face in the mirror.

Rabbit Redux is the second and most controversial in the series of novels about Harry Angstrom. The success of *Rabbit Run* in 1960 turned into a curse and a challenge for Updike. "I got sick of people talking about Rabbit, sick of them asking me what happened to him. So I decided to revisit my old friend."[3] Harry Angstrom is ten years older in *Rabbit Redux*, and it is only the author who still calls him "Rabbit." Harry is no longer the irresponsible drifter of the first novel; he has returned to his wife and child—the very title means "Rabbit led back"—and they live together in a suburban house. The restless,

wandering, unfaithful Harry has turned into a middle-aged conservative who supports the war in Vietnam and fears the evidence of a
changing America. Updike wrote the novel, he tells us, when "the
Sixties pressed heavily upon me," and the social turmoil so obvious at
the end of the decade speaks from every page of the book.

Although he has experimented with myth and parable in novels like *The Centaur* and *A Month of Sundays*, Updike does expect his art
to render a specific witness of contemporary life. "My fiction about the
daily doings of ordinary people has more history in it than history
books."[4] The critics, however, who try to explain the images of history
that appear in Updike's fiction often become unfairly reductive. Many
of the characters in *Rabbit Redux* can be discussed as familiar types
from the late 1960s: Harry comes from the silent majority of the Nixon
era, Jill is "into" drugs and radical politics to demonstrate her rejection
of the "system" represented by her rich parents, and Skeeter has
returned from Vietnam as a vengeful, drug-dealing, black militant.
The types are familiar enough, but history is more than stereotypes,
and Updike's fiction is not a series of clichés. If his art brings together
history and fiction, the common element is metaphor, and Updike's
success in *Rabbit Redux* can be measured by his use of metaphors from
the contemporary experience of Apollo 11 and Vietnam.

Not only does Updike expect his audience to appreciate the
historical accuracy of his fiction, he also asks for a consideration of
moral questions. "My books are all meant to be moral debates with the
reader, and if they seem pointless . . . it's because the reader has not
been engaged in the debate." How can Updike hope to engage readers
or critics who have been educated in schools ranging from New
Criticism to Post-Structuralism? Despite their differences, most critical theories for more than two generations have discounted the idea of
a novelist claiming to be a moralist. Just when critics are prepared
with the latest tools for deconstructing sign systems, Updike raises the
oldest moral issues: "The question is usually, 'What is a good man?' or
'What is goodness?' and in all the books an issue is examined."
Imagine the voice of Socrates suddenly coming from the pages of *The
New Yorker*!

Updike may expect his work to invoke the concerns of history
and morality, but oddly enough it has been condemned for a lack of
such content. The preciosity of his style may have convinced some
readers that Updike is content to probe deeply into the surface of

things. Norman Mailer, for example, declares that whenever Updike is uncertain about the direction of a novel—"he cultivates his private vice, he *writes*."[5] Who could know more about this vice than Mailer himself! The most extreme statement of the view—"Mr. Updike has nothing to say."—is made by John W. Aldridge in *Time to Murder and Create: The Contemporary Novel in Crisis*.[6]

Rabbit Redux takes place during the spring and fall of 1969 when the two events which dominate the headlines are the voyage of Apollo 11 and the trauma of Vietnam. While the events are documented by Mailer in separate books, *Of A Fire On The Moon* and *Why We Are In Vietnam*, Updike brings them together to form the background of his novel. The separation of history and fiction in the two sections of Mailer's *The Armies of the Night*—the subtitle of the book is "History as a Novel, The Novel as History"—is some measure of the double vision Updike had to reckon with in the late '60s. His solution to the problem is the opposite of Mailer's. Instead of separating history and fiction, Updike creates dramatic characters who respond to one another in a context of current events. Harry and Janice Angstrom must cope with their jealousy, fear, lust, and frustration while the television screen reveals Americans walking on the moon and napalming Vietnam.

From time to time the fictional characters may discuss the public events, but Updike usually allows the television to speak for itself. The result is not a commentary on history but rather a novel with fictional characters who are firmly rooted in the historical present. The characters may not be able to make sense of the news on television, at times they neither comprehend nor care about the far side of the earth or the moon, but they cannot escape the sights and sounds of soldiers and astronauts.

The flight of Apollo 11 proved to be an inspiration for several books in the early 1970s. Norman Mailer pretends to give us the most realistic account, but the vanity of the author often obscures the view. Many facts and figures about Apollo 11 are offered, but *Of A Fire On The Moon* is still limited and unreliable. The flight to the moon was also on Saul Bellow's mind as he wrote *Mr. Sammler's Planet*, but the idea of space travel is treated in a comic fashion when the original title— "The Future of the Moon"—is shifted to the work of a minor character. John Updike's many references to Apollo 11 in *Rabbit Redux* are less sensational than the words of Mailer, and less controversial than the opinions of Bellow's comic scientist, but finally more satisfying than either.

Mailer's book has the advantage of journalistic immediacy. He visits the NASA facilities in Houston and Cape Kennedy. He interviews the astronauts. He even has dinner with Wernher von Braun. The summer of 1969 is recreated for us with all of the sights and sounds of press briefings, motel rooms for journalists, and full immersion into the jargon of space technology. Mailer and Updike are both fascinated by the language used by the astronauts, and each will include several examples of their mechanical speech. Mailer tries to analyze the psychology of these men who are programmed like robots, while Updike faithfully gives us their words and maneuvers on the television screen. Mailer has the advantage of being present at Cape Kennedy when the astronauts lift off for the moon, and his prose description of the moment echoes the fire and thrust of the scene. *Of A Fire On The Moon* contains some of Mailer's best writing. The book, however, is marred by the vain posturing of Mailer the Philosopher. Seldom content just to describe an event, Mailer has to wrestle with the language until he wrings out some philosophical meaning. Thus we are told that launching rockets to the moon may be the ultimate gesture of America in the role of Faust. Should we label the rockets "pride," "hubris," and "vanity"? Should we look for the jaws of hell on the far side of the moon? Damnation always sells books, but Mailer could spare us the sophomoric rhetoric. The space program may well be a dangerous ego trip for America, but more often than not Mailer appears to confuse his own appetite for power and glory with his vision of the national purpose. Dinner with Wernher von Braun indeed!

Saul Bellow's ironic response to the success of Apollo 11 has already been noted. The scientist in Bellow's novel appears blind to real human needs, and his wish to plant colonies on the moon is finally revealed to be vain and futile. The manuscript of the scientist may be entitled "The Future of the Moon," but in *Mr. Sammler's Planet* the manuscript is comically stolen, twice lost, and never published. Bellow thus compromises the lunar hopes with his indirect comedy.

Updike's strategy is more straightforward and yet more difficult to analyze. He neither intrudes with his own philosophical comments in the vein of Mailer, nor does he create a comic advocate for the space program to match Bellow's scientist. Instead, he works the language of space exploration into the very texture of his novel.

Each of the four chapters of *Rabbit Redux* is prefixed with a quote from the conversation of Americans or Russians in space. At the beginning of Chapter One we hear two cosmonauts describe the maneuver of linking capsules in space: "It took me quite a while to find you, but now I've got you."[7] This linking operation will be used as a sexual metaphor throughout the novel, but in the first chapter it is especially important because it took Janice Angstrom quite a while to find a partner for adultery, and now she feels the victory of "I've got you." It was Harry Angstrom in *Rabbit Run* who strayed from his wife into the arms of Ruth, but in the sequel the situation is reversed. For ten years Harry has been faithful if not very passionate, and it is Janice who seeks fulfillment with a used car salesman.

Harry learns about his wife's affair on the same day that Apollo 11 lifts off for the moon. Harry's father tells him the gossip about Janice while the television in the bar "for the twentieth time that day" shows the rocket blasting off. It is typical of Updike to place the mundane unhappiness of his fictional characters against the mindless repetition of television news. His description of the moon launch couldn't be further removed from the dramatic observation of Mailer at Cape Kennedy. Updike describes the men in the bar watching the rocket as if it were a "tall kettle" with steam boiling underneath. Instead of Mailer's ecstatic response to the lift-off, Updike merely reports: "The men dark along the bar murmur among themselves. They have not been lifted, they are left here" (7). What can the exploration of space mean to these men at the bar? A new frontier for American heroes? Hardly. The men watch television at the Phoenix Bar which is decorated with fake western images. No power will lift them from their pseudo frontier of neon cowgirls and faded cactuses.

Harry comes home to find his wife absent and his teenage son talking about the rocket launch. Neither subject seems to him open to control or comprehension. Harry then eats his TV dinner while watching the six o'clock news. The report is naturally "all about space, all about emptiness." The commentators talk about the flight to the moon in terms of Columbus discovering the New World, "but as far as Rabbit can see it's the exact opposite: Columbus flew blind and hit something, these guys see exactly where they're aiming and it's a big round nothing" (22). Reducing the astronauts to "these guys" is typical of the deflation that occurs in this novel. If the moon is a "round nothing" and space is all "emptiness," the voyage of the astronauts will reveal no more than Harry already feels within himself. Like the speaker of Frost's poem he is unmoved by the "empty spaces/Between stars" because he knows too well his own "desert places."

Harry operates a linotype machine for the newspaper of a small city. The headline for this week reads: "BREWER FACTORY TOOLS COMPONENT HEADED TOWARD MOON." Harry tries to set the type correctly even though he knows the story is foolish and the newspaper is superfluous. Updike identifies a bit with his fictional character—"the way Rabbit sits in front of his linotype machine day after day reminded me of myself, of the way I sit in front of the typewriter"—and the character thus can be seen as a simplified portrait of the artist.

Harry often thinks in terms of newsprint, and Updike exploits this as a stylistic device to present the interior monologue. Several of Harry's mistakes at the linotype machine are included in the text of the novel to give us an impression of his distracted mind. His effort to arrange thoughts in a linear sequence proves increasingly difficult. "He put his life into rules he feels melting away now" (53). The rules for linear sequence are abandoned when the daily news comes direct from the television. The result is a loss of the very words that his linotype machine is supposed to arrange. "All around him, Rabbit hears language collapsing" (150). In the last chapter of the novel he loses his job as a linotype operator. The images from the television, the moonchild and the black veteran, have come alive in his living room, and the skills of the typesetter have become obsolete.

Near the end of the first chapter Harry is visiting his parents and the astronauts are landing on the moon. His father of course is watching the television and calls out with a voice of borrowed triumph: "They're down! Eagle has landed! . . . Uncle Sam is on the moon!" His mother replies with her usual scorn: "That's just the place for him" (93). It is the mother's birthday, and she knows that it will probably be her last. The family conversation, forlorn and nostalgic, is interspersed with voices which come via television from mission control in Houston and the astronauts on the moon. At the end of the evening the first lunar steps are reported: "At last it happens. The real event. Or is it? A television camera on the leg of the module comes on: an abstraction appears on the screen" (99). By this time Harry's father and son have both fallen asleep. What is the real event? Nothing done by the astronauts in their white suits. Harry can only think of his wife's desertion. "I know it's happened," he says at the very end of the chapter, "but I don't feel anything yet." His sense of loss is one with the emptiness of space. Janice has taken her first step away from him, and he thinks of his house as an empty spacecraft—"a long empty box in the blackness of Penn Villas, slowly spinning in the void."

The second chapter begins with the words of Neil Armstrong on the moon: "It's different but it's very pretty out here." The inadequacy of such a statement is precisely what attracts Updike. Harry Angstrom has been criticized as a dull specimen of middle America, a representative of the silent majority, but compared to the astronauts with their mechanical and vapid speech, Harry is almost intelligent. While the Eagle lands at Tranquility Base, and Armstrong puts the American flag on the moon, Harry's unfaithful wife drives away in their Falcon with a flag decal on the rear window. What can Harry do about this turn of affairs? Ten years ago in *Rabbit Run* he would have tried to escape. But now Harry is thirty-six; he has a teenage son to worry about; and he wants to make sense out of the pieces of his life. Instead of trying to shield himself from the hurt pride of the cuckold, Harry keeps looking in the mirror as if he were fascinated with his own horns. Perhaps he blames himself because he was the first to break the vows of marriage. The guilt and despair mixed in with his jealousy make Harry feel numb and ineffectual.

His passive submission to the major events of the novel—the infidelity of Janice, the demands of Jill and Skeeter, and the destruction of his house—has been taken as evidence that Harry Angstrom is essentially weak and hopeless. It is true that he often gives himself a low grade—"As a human being I'm about C minus."—but Harry is neither a fool nor a coward, and it is a common mistake to underestimate his character. Critics have called him "a kind of post World War II nobody" and "the quintessence of the non hero," but Updike knows better than to place a nonentity at the center of three novels.[8] Harry may not travel to the moon and back, but he is busy exploring the space inside of the heart. If the moon is traditionally associated with love and madness, it may be that Updike's protagonist learns more about both of these subjects than either Armstrong or Aldrin with their footprints in the moon dust.

Harry's exploration of love and madness is made possible by Jill and Skeeter, the title characters of chapters two and three respectively, who suddenly enter the void of Harry's life and show him the dark phases of the moon. Jill has been tempted away from the home of her rich parents to try the forbidden fruit of radical politics and a self-destructive life style. Drugs and sex are never enough to satisfy her moon-crazed senses. Harry gives her the shelter of his home, but eventually the girl and the house will be destroyed in flames. Harry also gives shelter to Skeeter who thinks of himself as a black Jesus, and then Harry must cope with his rage and madness.

The second chapter largely dramatizes what Harry learns from the "moonchild." Jill is too young to be a replacement for Janice, and too old to take the place of Angstrom's lost daughter, but she does arouse both desire and tenderness in Harry. Jill knows more about sex and drugs than Harry expects, but she also has the vulnerability of a teenager, and Harry wants to protect her. Jill's entry into Harry's life is a jolt to his routine and a challenge to his latent idealism. When she begins to live in the house the television is silenced. Instead of watching the six o'clock news, she wants to "discuss God, beauty, meaning" (158). Her idealism is the other side of her self-destructive fury—in either case she refuses to accept the world as it is—and both halves of her personality draw Harry from his passive retreat.

Near the end of the chapter when Harry feels "this unique summer, this summer of the moon, slipping away forever," he asks her if she wouldn't like to "make love." When they lie together on the floor Updike describes the empty television screen as "a mother-planet above them." At the climax of their passion "moonchild and earth-man" move in the same orbit. The double reputation of the moon as a goddess of virgins and a patron of lunatics may be as old as literature, but Updike brings together ancient myth and modern space exploration in a new way to create the metaphors and life of his fiction.

At the beginning of the third chapter Updike quotes a cosmonaut aboard Soyuz 5: "We've been raped, we've been raped!" This unexpected communication from space is most appropriate for the chapter of *Rabbit Redux* which begins with the sudden appearance of Skeeter and ends with the violent death of Jill. It is a chapter filled with the politics of revolution and Skeeter's language of evangelical violence. Skeeter sees himself as a black Jesus, and his image of Vietnam as the Second Coming rivals Yeats's rough beast in its gratuitous horror: "Chaos is His holy face. The sun is burning through. The moon is turning red. The moon is a baby's head bright red between his momma's legs" (261-262). Updike thus brings together the moon and the war imagery to underscore the historical immediacy of Skeeter's vision. The turning gyres appear to intersect during the summer and fall of 1969—"It is the end. It is the beginning."—as the television screens repeatedly show the craters of the moon and the scarred landscape of Vietnam. But the child of violence sprung from this unhappy conjunction is Skeeter himself—the rough beast who is drugged with the madness of war and wants to possess the blood red moon.

At first Harry tries to dismiss Skeeter's mixture of religion and war. "It's just a dirty little war that has to be fought. You can't make something religious out of it just because you happened to be there" (262). But after awhile Harry realizes that the war has made something out of Skeeter; it has made him into the agent of violence and destruction who advertises himself as "the Christ of the new Dark Age." Despite his conviction that the gospel according to Skeeter is bad news, Harry is unable to prevent the disaster. Fire and flood are the Biblical judgments that he cannot escape. Ten years earlier his infant daughter was accidently drowned. Now the drug-crazed Jill will be burned to death in his suburban home. Harry not only has to witness the horror of the fire, afterwards he must help the black Jesus slip away from the police. At the end of the chapter Harry drives Skeeter out of town until they reach an intersection with a sign pointing the few miles to Galilee.

Several critics have complained about the religious symbolism in *Rabbit Redux*. Eugene Lyons, for example, is scornful of Updike's presentation of Skeeter: "Perhaps he is the Antichrist. It is almost as difficult to know as it is to care."[9] Updike himself complains in an interview that no critic has "given serious consideration to the idea that Skeeter, the angry black, might *be* Jesus. He *says* he is. I think probably he might be."[10] At least one critic has thrown up his hands in despair: "Seldom, if ever, has any white writer been paralyzed into sentimental and self-contradictory blather quite so foolish in attempting to deal with a black character."[11] When a critic is moved to protest so loudly, it is usually an inverse compliment to the boldness of the author. Updike indeed is bold to suggest a black Jesus in *Rabbit Redux*. First, he has to create a convincing voice that mixes ghetto slang and evangelical violence. Skeeter must talk with the authority of the dark side of the moon and the scarred battlefields of Vietnam. Second, the character has to be established as an apocalyptic agent who has sprung from the chaos of contemporary events. "This was an era when we lived by television," Updike explains, and Skeeter "just came in off the set into Rabbit's lap."[12] And third, if Updike wants to suggest the return of Christ, the character has to be convincing as a religious nightmare. The rough beast is last seen in the novel slouching towards Galilee. Skeeter certainly ranks among the more daring experiments in contemporary literature. If his presentation is not wholly success-ful, perhaps it is because the realistic base of the novel will not fully support the strain of the religious and apocalyptic. But the real voice of the cosmonaut at the beginning of the chapter—"We've been raped, we've been raped!"—should warn us that the news from outer space is not what we expect.

The death of Skeeter is reported ten years later in *Rabbit is Rich*. He is shot by police officers who have come to investigate his religious commune known as the Messiah Now Freedom Family. After his death signs begin mysteriously to appear on walls about town that proclaim "Skeeter lives." Harry may feel safer with Skeeter gone, but now in middle age he is left with the banal gods of sex and money. The third novel in the series only has a few echoes of the radical politics and religious madness so much a part of its predecessor.

The final chapter of *Rabbit Redux* begins with the matter-of-fact conversation in which Aldrin is attempting to guide Armstrong out of the spacecraft to begin his walk on the surface of the moon. Updike introduces a similar guide who is able to bring Harry and Janice back together at the Safe Haven Motel. It is Harry's sister, a Las Vegas call girl, who helps him to question and understand his own conduct. Early in the novel he wanted to prevent the seeds of the devil from "taking over the garden," but eventually he comes to understand that "all things must fall." This is the knowledge he gains from his space exploration of the heart.

The fall from innocence is often construed by American au-thors as the failure of the American dream. Updike is no exception, and *Rabbit Redux* has been noted for representing "the disintegrating quality of American life in the 1960s" and "the loss of the American dream."[13] Harry Angstrom has been described as "an American Adam fallen and unredeemed."[14] If imitations of Adam seem to multiply at an alarming rate in contemporary American literature, it may be the fault of R. W. B. Lewis's persuasive *The American Adam*. Since the appearance of his critical study in 1955 the images of a fallen world have become even more familiar, and Updike does echo several of them. His candidate for Adam likes to recall "decades when Americans moved within the American Dream . . . the national anthem everywhere," and then he laments "the world shrank like an apple going bad" (124). *Rabbit Redux* is filled with the taste of the forbidden fruit: sex and death in the fallen world. The sex of Jill and Skeeter and Harry—"O.K., strip and get into it, she's full of holes, right?"—is described like the congress of the damned. The violent death of Jill adds a meaningless casualty to the landscape of war zones and moon craters.

Updike may be an expert when it comes to projecting images of a fallen world, but his mentors are more European than American. Proust and Nabokov are the acknowledged models for the kind of nostalgia which Updike attempts to represent. "Only three or four books in a lifetime," Swann says in *Remembrance of Things Past*, "give us anything that is of real importance." Updike was twenty-three when he began to read Proust—"it was a revelation to me that words could entwine and curl so, yet keep a live crispness and the breath of utterance."[15] Not only is Updike's style clearly influenced by Proust, he also learned how to delineate a lost paradise in the entwined and curling echo chamber of a character's memory. Updike has also praised Nabokov's *Speak Memory* for its "metaphorical arabesques, the floral rhythms, and the immobilized surrender to memory."[16] The same words of praise could be applied to *Rabbit Redux*. Updike claims that "only an expatriate Russian . . . can know nostalgia so exquisite," but his own achievement with the character of Harry Angstrom is a tribute to Proust and Nabokov.

The lost paradise of Updike's hero is represented by memories of his youth. He likes to dream about the happy days when he was a star basketball player. After the fire he moves back into his parent's house, and his old surroundings induce a flood of nostalgia. When his sister returns it almost seems to him as if the past were about to begin again. He even starts to wear his old high school athletic jacket. The very title of the novel, of course, suggests that the protagonist will be led back. But nostalgia just isn't what it used to be. Harry has learned to look at his boyhood surroundings with the eyes of a fallen man: "There was a time . . . when this homely street . . . excited Rabbit with the magic of his own existence. These mundane surfaces had given witness to his life; this chalice had held his blood; here the universe had centered, each downtwirling maple seed of more account than galaxies. No more" (373).

After years of attempting to resist time by living with memory and nostalgia, Harry has finally learned that: "Time is our element, not a mistaken invader" (374). The acceptance of time is another way for him to admit the loss of paradise. Harry and Janice have no home to return to at the end of the novel, but "hand in hand with wandering steps and slow" they hesitantly search for a motel. Janice has put an empty suitcase in the car just in case. When they stop at a place that advertises "ALL COLOR TVS" and "MAGIC FINGERS" their life together in the fallen world is about to begin. "In a space of silence . . . he feels them drift along sideways deeper into being married" (405). The summer of the moon is over. The fall of Vietnam is inevitable. Updike has fulfilled his promise to give specific witness to moral issues and contemporary history. But the moon and the war have been metaphors of exploration and combat in the heart of man. Updike's novel therefore ends with the discovery that: "The space they are in . . . becomes all interior space."

Notes

[1] John Updike, *Picked-Up Pieces* (New York: Alfred A. Knopf, 1975), p. 31.

[2] Suzanne Uphaus, *John Updike* (New York: Frederick Ungar, 1980), p. 80, and Eugene Lyons, "John Updike: The Beginning and the End," *Critique*, vol. 14, no. 2 (1972), p. 44.

[3] John Updike, *Picked-Up Pieces*, p. 510.

[4] *Ibid.*, p. 501.

[5] Norman Mailer, *Cannibals and Christians* (New York: Dial, 1966), p. 120.

[6] John W. Aldridge, *Time to Murder and Create: The Contemporary Novel in Crisis* (New York: David McKay Company, 1964), p. 170.

[7] John Updike, *Rabbit Redux* (New York: Alfred A. Knopf, 1971), p. 2. All further references to this edition are cited parenthetically.

[8] Wayne Falke, "*Rabbit Redux*: Time/Order/God," *Modern Fiction Studies*, vol. 20, no. 1 (Spring, 1974), p. 62, and Robert Detweiler, *John Updike* (Boston:

Twayne, 1972), p. 50.

⁹ Eugene Lyons, "John Updike: The Beginning and the End," *Critique*, p. 57.

¹⁰ John Updike, *Picked-Up Pieces*, p. 510.

¹¹ Eugene Lyons, pp. 57-58.

¹² John Updike letter to George W. Hunt, July 9, 1979, quoted in George W. Hunt, *John Updike and the three great secret things: Sex, Religion, and Art* (Grand Rapids: William B. Eerdmans Company, 1980), p. 171.

¹³ Robert Detweiler, *John Updike*, p. 158, and Wayne Falke, "*Rabbit Redux*: Time/Order/God," *Modern Fiction Studies*, p. 59.

¹⁴ George W. Hunt, *John Updike and the three great secret things: Sex, Religion, and Art*, p. 165.

¹⁵ John Updike, *Picked-Up Pieces*, p. 163.

¹⁶ *Ibid.*, p. 192.

1972

Margaret Atwood
Surfacing

Displayed on the cedar wall above Margaret Atwood's desk are the words of Franz Kafka: "A book must be like an ice-axe to break the sea frozen inside us." From her first book of poems, *Double Persephone* (1961), to her latest novel, *Cat's Eye* (1988), Atwood has done more than break the surface of that frozen sea, she has followed several avatars of Persephone into the underworld. *Surfacing* is Atwood's best narrative of the descent and return of the mythical heroine. Hailed by the *New York Times Book Review* as "one of the most important novels in the twentieth century," *Surfacing* has attracted wide critical attention, and lately has been described as a "quest classic."[1] Atwood herself is not happy with such labels, but at least she would agree that the word "quest" implies both a literary form and the challenge of Kafka to "break the sea frozen inside us."

"Romance is the structural core of all fiction," claims Northrop Frye, "it brings us closer than any other aspect of literature to the sense of fiction . . . man's vision of his own life as a quest."[2] Despite its acceptance as a narrative quest, Atwood's novel still demands a variety of critical approaches. Some readers have described the book as a quest for spiritual vision, while others see the goal as psychological knowledge. Some feel the novel is a quest for national identity, others for feminist power. Perhaps the most interesting critical approach is to analyse the archetypal form which serves as the basis for the narrative quest. Atwood follows the basic patterns of comedy and romance familiar in Shakespearean drama. What novel in recent years has attracted such a variety of readers and interpreters?[3] If the 1970s are remarkable for the increasing symbiosis of popular fiction and academic criticism, Margaret Atwood's *Surfacing* is rightly the *cause célèbre* of the decade.

The critical hunt for religious symbols is the least convincing. The narrator of *Surfacing* has been taught by her father to think of Christianity as irrational and unnecessary. Although she felt deprived of religious knowledge as a child, and at times curious about it, the narrator has remained independent. Seldom does she use metaphors that are explicitly Christian. The most famous is her meditation on the dead heron—"anything that suffers and dies instead of us is Christ"—but this has more to do with how she feels about victims than with any significant faith.

Not caring much for the type of god that would allow human sacrifice, especially the crucifixion of his own son, the narrator is more interested in the protective spirits of nature. Her father left copies of Indian rock paintings which may have a religious meaning. "The Indians did not own salvation, but . . . their signs marked the sacred places, the places where you could learn the truth."[4] The narrator tries to find the rock paintings by following the map and drawings prepared by her father. The search leads to her father's corpse, and beyond that to a period of madness when the commands of the Indian gods appear to be directing her conduct. If this is a religious quest, it takes her paradoxically into a "state of nature" where she lives for awhile like an animal in a lair. At the end of the novel the gods of nature are silent and unyielding—"The lake is quiet, the trees surround me, asking and giving nothing."

The plot of *Surfacing* is more often explained as a psychological journey. The narrator's search for her dead father is typically described as a quest for her own identity. R. D. Laing's definition of psychotherapy—"the paring away of all that stands between us, the props, the masks, roles, lies, defenses, anxieties, projections and interjections"—is a fair account of Atwood's narrative strategy.[5] The psychological history of the narrator who speaks in the first person is revealed in a series of dramatic confessions. The truth of her abortion gradually breaks through the surface of the lies and masks that have been her defense.

Margaret Atwood herself has been in psychoanalysis, and she is particularly fond of using metaphors to dramatize the unconscious. Even the titles of her poems, "Journey Towards the Interior" or "Procedures for Underground," betray this psychological interest.

When she describes the latter poem as "a descent to the underworld," she knows the value of the metaphor. Thus it is hardly a surprise to find the narrator of *Surfacing* dive beneath the surface of the lake to discover the body of her father. The sight of the corpse underwater proves to be the shock required to bring the image of her aborted fetus into consciousness and thus beyond the repressive control of guilt or fear. One dive into the unconscious thus frees the narrator from both father and unborn child. She also emerges from her psychological descent without the feeling of death which had been left after the abortion: "I'd carried that death around inside me, layering it over, a cyst, a tumor, black pearl" (165). Atwood's narrator is the most dramatic heroine to face the roots of desire in the dark forest since Hester Prynne, and it is entirely suitable that her unborn child of adultery should be called a "black pearl."

As long as the narrator of *Surfacing* carries the feeling of death at the bottom of her psyche, she is unable to feel any life or love for the man who wants to marry her. Through most of the novel she regards Joe as if he were an object and not a person. "When he suggested we should live together I didn't hesitate. It wasn't even a real decision, it was more like buying a goldfish or a potted cactus plant" (47). The narrator complains that her head and heart have been separated. She even imagines herself as the woman sawed in half during a magic show. The goal of her psychological quest is therefore a reunification of self, and this is typically achieved by the descent into the underworld of repressed feeling and death. Only when the narrator comes to the surface again is she able to welcome the passion of Joe, and then the black pearl of death is replaced in her womb by a seed promising new life.

The popularity of Atwood's novel has much to do with the illusion it projects of the successful psychological quest. The narrator does not emerge from the underworld like the hero of Conrad's novel unable to shake the darkness or to escape new lies. Instead, she feels released from the shadows of guilt and prepared to accept the future. The psychological journey described in Frost's "Directive" is apparently completed by Atwood's heroine: "Here are your waters and your watering place./Drink and be whole again beyond confusion."

The new identity of the narrator may also be understood in national terms. *Surfacing* may be read as a celebration of the renaissance of Canadian literature. Atwood's narrator uses the word

"American" for almost anything that appears to threaten her identity. The label is also applied to all who come to the wilderness to catch the fish or hunt the animals. "It doesn't matter what country they're from, my head said, they're still Americans" (148). The narrator feels threatened by a form of evil which takes over the land and the body "like a virus." The signs of the growing disease show up in the wilderness as paved roads, motor boats, commercial projects, and whatever proves the threat of encroaching civilization. The question for the narrator is how to avoid the fate of the dead heron. Near the end of the novel she rejects the few comforts of her father's cabin, and chooses to survive for awhile in a state of nature. Complete identification with the hunted animals is the beginning of her cure for the virus of a foreign civilization.

Survival is seen by Atwood as the principal theme of Canadian literature, and that is the title she used for a guidebook to her nation's literature which she also published in 1972. *Survival* includes the rationale for the national theme in *Surfacing*. Atwood does not hesitate to see the patterns of literature as "a reflection of a national habit of mind."[6] She identifies the frontier as the basic symbol of American literature, and because the very existence of a frontier depends upon its constant expansion, the result is what Atwood calls "the general imperialism of the American cast of mind."[7] The usual defense against imperialism is to assert the rights and feelings of a native culture. The growth of Atwood's career coincides with an amazing renaissance of Canadian literature. Not only do her own poems and novels explore the concerns of national identity, her guidebook to Canadian literature offers a map of the literary territory. *Survival* is a book written by a poet and novelist who does not hesitate to reflect broadly on the form and content of her national culture. If imperialism is the American consequence of having to maintain the illusion of a frontier, then fear of becoming a victim is the natural Canadian response. If the hero of American literature from Melville to Hemingway is often the hunter, then it makes sense for Atwood to identify Canadian literature with the feelings of the victim.

The fundamental question is asked by the narrator of *Surfacing*—why must the hunting and killing continue? If her first answer is to see the animals as sacrificial victims—"the animals die that we may live"—the secret of survival is to move beyond the role of the victim. Atwood's novel dramatizes that movement. At the beginning the narrator does identify with the animals. Indeed, she thinks of her father as a fish and her mother as a bird. Moreover, the part of herself that has been killed, the fetus that has been aborted, is described as "an animal . . . hiding in me as if in a burrow." The narrator follows this identification to its limit when she removes her clothes and curls up like an animal in "a lair near the woodpile." After this wild perform-ance she is finally ready to leave the natural state, and "above all, to refuse to be a victim." The new life suggested at the end is the renaissance of Canadian literature. Atwood's novel thus projects the successful quest for national identity.

Another interpretation of the quest has been in terms of femi-nist power. The relationship of Anna and David lends the novel a background of sexual warfare: "she was fighting for her life . . . if she ever surrendered the balance of power would be broken and he would go elsewhere" (175). The war continues because Anna and David are afraid of self-knowledge. Without the comfort and distraction of cosmetics, cigarettes, and daily baseball scores, Anna and David would have to face themselves. The narrator is the only character with the courage to dive into the lake because she alone is prepared to cope with the fear and guilt of the unconscious. Anna and David live on the surface where the battle of the sexes continues with each threatening to throw the other into the water. Perhaps for them the novel should be called: "Fear of Diving." The only way to reach the self-knowledge gained by the narrator is to plunge into the darkness of the lake. Atwood describes the narrator's dive as a test of will and courage: "My spine whipped, I hit the water and kicked myself down, sliding through the lake strata, gray to darker gray, cool to cold" (161). In this way she finds the corpse of her father and the image of her unborn child, and both together are the truth that set her free. Her successful quest for full identity as a woman has undoubtedly helped the narrator of *Surfacing* to become one of the most highly regarded heroines in contemporary literature.

The archetypal significance of the quest has been the focus of several critics who are mindful of the religious, psychological, na-tional, and feminist interpretations, but prefer to explore the underly-ing patterns of myth.[8] The results vary depending on whether the guiding spirit is Joseph Campbell, Marcea Eliade, Northrop Frye, or Carl Jung. The principle however remains the same. The narrator of *Surfacing* is shown to re-enact a pattern from mythology—a ritual journey of descent and rebirth.

Margaret Atwood's interest in such patterns is explored in an essay she wrote just prior to her novel.[9] Forms of literary criticism, she argues, are shaped by national concerns. American critics tend to focus on literary technique; English critics tend to worry about matters of taste; and Canadian writers may typically concern themselves with an abstract design or synthesis. This is no doubt true of Atwood's friend and mentor, Northrop Frye, and it applies as well to her own critical method. Indeed, the synthesis described in *Survival* is developed from the categories of the earlier essay. American critics are interested in technique because the notion of "how to do it" is the most important for the frontier. The English critic is more concerned with taste because the great works are in the past and they must be kept alive as implicit standards. Uncommitted to either national focus, the Canadian critic is therefore free to create a synthesis. Books like Frye's *Anatomy of Criticism*, McLuhan's *Understanding Media*, and Atwood's *Survival* are the result. Given this critical context it is neither surprising that Atwood's first collection of poems should be entitled *Double Persephone*, nor remarkable that archetypal patterns inform much of her fiction.

The mythic pattern of *Surfacing* is familiar enough: the descent into the underworld, a meeting with the shadow of death, a madness to become one with nature, and a return to the surface with new control, power, and wholeness. Where does the basic design of this story come from? Examples can be found scattered among several primitive societies. The chief figure of this type in classical mythology is Persephone, and variations on the central theme are endless. The Eleusinian mysteries raise the story to the level of faith and ritual. Epic literature, whether Greek, Roman, or Christian, typically includes a trip to the underworld and the promised return.

The story of Persephone has been retold by Shakespeare, Milton, Shelley, Keats, Swinburne, etc. Its appeal to a primitive people whose visions of life and death must follow the rhythm of the seasons is not hard to understand. Persephone, after all, is the daughter of the chief goddess of agriculture and fertility. But why does the same mythic pattern continue to fascinate writers from Shakespeare to Swinburne? Does the human imagination repeatedly come back to the story because it delivers some deep-rooted psychological satisfaction? If the adventure in the underworld is a ritual contest with the shadow of death, then it may offer a way to cope with the most basic human fear. The promise of a return to the surface may then express the corresponding hope and desire. Atwood of course is well aware of the possibilities. She has read widely in mythology, epic literature, and archetypal criticism. She therefore finds herself at the crossroads of literature and myth. The time and place are right for the pattern of descent and renewal because the aspirations for a rebirth of Canadian literature, the renewed interest in the liberation of women, and the late twentieth century need to reaffirm the power of a vanishing nature may all be brought into focus with the archetypal story of Persephone.

Atwood's chief task is to stretch the literary conventions of a realistic novel to accommodate the mythic descent and return of a modern heroine. What can be used to represent the underworld? How can supernatural powers be invoked in a secular context? What can be done to save the heroine from the shadows of death? Atwood's solution is both realistic and still rich with primitive mystery. The journey to the underworld begins with a trip to a remote island on a lake in the Canadian wilderness. The narrator is traveling back in time and distance to the place of her childhood memories. The lake is both realistic and symbolic. When the narrator dives beneath the surface she does find the corpse of her father and the repressed image of her unborn child. The clues for her journey are the copies left by her father of the mysterious rock paintings done by the Indians. Their talismanic power opens a way for the secular narrator to experience the super-natural rules of the local deities. What appears near the end of the novel to be a realistic descent into madness is a response to the imaginary commands of the Indian gods. The madness includes a reunion of the narrator with her father and mother who both appear in the form of hallucinations. Thus the heroine is allowed to meet and transcend the shadows of death. At the end of the novel she is prepared to leave the island and the wilderness in order to begin a new life.

Atwood is able to bridge the distance from primitive myth to a realistic modern novel because she follows the basic patterns of comedy and romance which are the chief intervening literary forms. Rather than look to classical mythology or to epic narrative for a possible model, Atwood could see in the comedies and romances of Shakespeare how the ancient mythic patterns were already shaped into a dramatic form with a degree of realism. Strange things may happen to the characters in the wood near Athens or on the island controlled by Prospero, but at least the action must be represented on the stage. Once the patterns of myth have been turned into literary and dramatic conventions it is possible for a writer like Margaret Atwood to carry them further into modern fiction. Her novel follows a range of literature that begins with the comic design for *A Midsummer Night's Dream* and includes the romance design of *The Tempest*. The related patterns of comedy and romance share a visit to a natural world, a descent into romantic confusion, interference of the supernatural, and a return to the "real" world with promises of marriage and a new life.

A stubborn father and the harsh law of Athens cause the four young characters to enter the woods near the beginning of *A Midsummer Night's Dream*; a political misdeed in Milan sends Miranda and her father to the magic island in *The Tempest*; and the search for her father brings Atwood's narrator with three friends to the island in the Canadian backcountry. In each case the action of the play or novel moves into what Frye likes to call the "green world." The natural setting is a metaphor to dramatize the romantic and irrational depths of the human mind. The wood near Athens represents the dark forest of irrational desire in which the young characters fall comically in and out of love. The island in *The Tempest* is inhabited by a slave and a spirit who represent the extremes of human nature. The setting of Atwood's novel includes forest, island, and a lake which she readily explains "can be used as a metaphor for a descent into the unconscious."

At the heart of the comic design is the romantic confusion in the dark woods. The four characters in *Surfacing* often resemble the young lovers in Shakespeare's play. Their dialogue is filled with jealousy, desire, frustration, and vanity. Although two of the characters in the novel are married, their alliances still change with the caprice of sexual current. The tension and the confusion could not be greater if Puck were on the scene with his love potion. The jealous intrigue between Titania and Oberon serves as a dramatic convention to reveal the unpredictable nature of romantic desire. The transformation of Bottom into a comic ass, and his courtship by the queen of the fairy creatures, provide dramatic images for the absurd limits of unexpected passion. The narrator of *Surfacing* sees her potential lover as a threatened animal: "From the side he's like the buffalo on the U.S. nickel, shaggy and blunt-snouted, with small clenched eyes and the defiant but insane look of a species once dominant, now threatened with extinction" (8). She cannot respond to his pleas for love until she first comes to terms with the guilt and fear in her own psyche. The reason for entering the dark forest—the typical setting for a comic design—is to deal with the shadows which inhibit desire and to accept the animal face of nature. Atwood's narrator enters into the natural world far enough to be able to see her father and mother as the fish and the birds, discard her clothes, feed on wild plants, build herself a lair near the woodpile, and finally accept the new animal developing in her womb.

While the novel shows her progress in accepting the powers of nature, her companions have more difficulty in discarding their artificial habits—the baseball scores, the cosmetics, and the cigarettes. All they can accept is a parody of nature—the family of stuffed moose dressed in human clothes. Despite his anti-American rhetoric, David is really "a little boy moose in short pants, a striped jersey and baseball cap, waving an American flag" (14). If the "nature of the comic drive," as Northrop Frye explains, is "a drive toward identity," then it is only the narrator of *Surfacing* who achieves such a goal.[10]

Progress in a comic design is typically accomplished by the intervention of a supernatural power. Shakespeare's comedy includes a whole cast of fairy creatures with their magic tricks and potions. Atwood's novel includes the talismanic rock paintings of the Indians and the imagined commands of the local deities. Misadventures with the supernatural are common during the early scenes of a comic drama. The plot of *A Midsummer Night's Dream* is wildly complicated by the mischief and error of Puck. Atwood's narrator is confused at first when she mistakes the copies of rock paintings for drawings of madness. The experience of comedy for actors and audience alike is akin to the solving of a riddle. All of the clues revealed tend at first to create greater confusion, but eventually the pattern is clear, and the end is a celebration of symmetry.

"The mythical or primitive basis of comedy," according to Atwood's mentor, "is a movement toward the rebirth and renewal of the powers of nature."[11] This means of course the coming together of male and female. The symmetry of nature is the coupling of the sexes with the promise of creation. The traditional end of comedy is therefore the celebration of marriage. Three different couples in *A Midsummer Night's Dream* return from the dark forest for the wedding festival of Act V. Shakespeare's comic play and the wedding festival which it presents are both a ritual to celebrate the creative powers of human nature.

Atwood's novel does not end with wedding bells, but the fulfillment of the comic pattern is still sufficiently clear. The narrator and her lover are close together at the end, and she is thinking "we will have to begin." A few critics who find this ending less than conclusive have attempted to describe the whole closing chapter as ambivalent. One even goes so far as to suggest that what Atwood "really seems to be saying is that the mythical pattern . . . must itself be seen as a sham in a culture where rituals have lost their potency."[12] This is surely nonsense. If the mythic pattern is based on the symmetry of nature, then what evidence is there to prove that life or art has lost its potency? It is even possible that both may continue despite the critical search for ambivalence.

The narrative quest of *Surfacing* also follows the basic design of romance literature. Although this genre is close to comedy with a similar pattern of descent and return, there are some important differences. The formulas of romance place greater emphasis on the relationship of fathers and daughters, more concentration on the power of evil, and direct more attention to the shaping of a brave new world.

"In romance the descent theme," declares Frye, "is the discovery of the real relation between the chief characters and their parents."[13] Thus the long conversation between Miranda and Prospero in the second scene of *The Tempest*; or the search for a lost father in *Surfacing*. While the novel depicts a literal hunt for the missing parent, it also describes the attempt of the narrator to recover through memory the significance of her father. Atwood's heroine makes the descent into memory by returning to her childhood home and discovering the scrapbooks which she put together as a young girl. These contain her earliest record of her family relationships. Atwood's heroine also finds the notebooks of her father which are like the magic books of Prospero with their secrets of mysterious power. Only by deciphering the clues will she be led to the sacred places of the Indian gods, and thus to the actual discovery of her dead father. Although it is typical in romance for daughter and father to be reunited, the stress must fall on the ability of the daughter to survive her father. That is why Miranda is brought to the point in *The Tempest* of being prepared to inherit the brave new world, and Prospero is heard to say: "Every third thought shall be my grave." Once the narrator of *Surfacing* has visited the underwater grave of her father, she too is ready for the role of survivor.

The forces of evil are typically more important in romance than in comedy. Mischievous deeds occur in *A Midsummer Night's Dream*, but there are no characters with the murderous intentions of Antonio, Sebastian, or Caliban. The young lovers may be at odds with one another in the wood near Athens, jealousy and rash judgment are painful, but for the most part they are only in danger of making fools or asses of themselves. Prospero's island, however, is beset with foul conspiracies which threaten to kill the innocent and rape the virtuous. Only the magic power of Prospero is able to prevent tragedy. His power is often displayed by the supernatural tricks of Ariel, but it is based upon a moral vision of order and peace.

Atwood's narrator complains at first that she has not learned enough about evil from her father. He didn't warn her about selfish men, unwanted fetuses, and dead animals. He merely explained evil as irrational, and moved his family to the remote lake and island to express his pacifist nature. In such an environment the narrator still had to confront the animals killed by her brother, the fear of drowning in the lake, and the distant echoes of Hitler's war and destruction. "I didn't want there to be wars and death, I wanted them not to exist; only rabbits with their colored egg houses, sun and moon orderly above the flat earth, summer always, I wanted everyone to be happy" (151). The imagery here is from her childhood coloring book, but it suggests the wonder and innocence of Miranda who exclaims: "How many goodly creatures are there here!/How beauteous mankind is!" The task for the writer of romance is to preserve this sense of wonder beyond the knowledge of tragedy. Shakespeare allows Miranda to speak these words in the final scene of the play, although she has been fully informed of the evil history, and knows how to play the political game of chess. Atwood also forces her heroine to confront the many shapes of death: fish, heron, father, and unborn child, but still brings her to the final page of the novel where the most important words are "love" and "trust." The words have value at this time because the narrator has experienced love betrayed and trust exploited. After witnessing the power of evil she comes to appreciate the moral vision of her father who chose life over killing and learned how to find the signs of the natural gods.

The final vision of romance is more profoundly optimistic than the happy ending of comedy. In both there is the implied celebration of marriage, but in romance the couple is apt to be a prince and princess, and their union provides a basis for a new order of society. Miranda and Ferdinand at the end of *The Tempest* are ready to return to Naples where they will eventually rule over the brave new world. Thanks to the magic of Prospero they have even received a blessing from the goddesses of heaven and earth. The final scene includes the famous acknowledgment of a successful quest—"all of us [have found] ourselves/When no man was his own."

Atwood doesn't have a prince to offer her heroine, and the local gods are silent at the end, but the basic pattern of romance is still tentatively fulfilled. The narrator has made her descent into the natural world, gained her father's knowledge of evil and death, and returned to the surface with a renewed ability to love and trust. The man waiting for her at the end may be only "half formed," and she herself is hesitant, but their relationship is now beyond the confusion of the forest and the lake. Do they have a kingdom to inherit? The narrator has come to realize that her lover "isn't an American," and that means at least that both share the Canadian future of survival. The imaginative order of their new world is what Margaret Atwood describes in her next book. *Survival* is about the renaissance of Canadian literature which begins with the discovery of the creative energy in the designs of comedy and romance. The first novel of that renaissance ends with the narrator feeling inside herself the embryo of the brave new world—*Surfacing*.

Notes

[1] Francine du Plessix Gray, "Nature as Nunnery," *New York Times Book Review*, July 17, 1977, p. 29, and Arnold E. and Cathy N. Davidson, eds., *The Art of*

Margaret Atwood: Essays in Criticism (Toronto: Anansi, 1981), p. 13.

[2] Northrop Frye, *The Secular Scripture: A Study of the Structure of Romance* (Cambridge: Harvard University Press, 1976), p. 15.

[3] See the bibliography compiled by Alan J. Horne in *The Art of Margaret Atwood: Essays in Criticism.*

[4] Margaret Atwood, *Surfacing* (New York: Simon and Schuster, 1972), p. 166. All further references to this edition are cited parenthetically.

[5] R. D. Laing, *Politics of Experience* (New York: Random House, 1967), pp. 46-47.

[6] Margaret Atwood, *Survival: A Thematic Guide to Canadian Literature* (Toronto: Anansi, 1972), p. 13.

[7] *Ibid.*, p. 74.

[8] See Annis Pratt, "*Surfacing* and the Rebirth Journey," *The Art of Margaret Atwood: Essays in Criticism*, pp. 139-157, and Barbara H. Rigney, "After the Failure of Logic: Descent and Return in *Surfacing*," *Madness and Sexual Politics in the Feminist Novel* (Madison: University of Wisconsin Press, 1978), pp. 91-127.

[9] See "Eleven Years of *Alphabet*," *Canadian Literature*, No. 49 (Summer 1971), pp. 60-64.

[10] Northrop Frye, *A Natural Perspective: The Development of Shakespearean Comedy and Romance* (New York: Columbia University Press, 1965), p. 118.

[11] *Ibid.*, p. 119.

[12] Robert Lecker, "Janus through the Looking Glass: Atwood's First Three Novels," *The Art of Margaret Atwood: Essays in Criticism*, p. 194.

[13] Northrop Frye, *The Secular Scripture: A Study of the Structure of Romance*, p. 122.

1973

Kurt Vonnegut
Breakfast of Champions

What happens when an author becomes a character in his own fiction? The charge of narcissism has often been leveled against the culture of the 1970s, and the decade is remarkable for the many novelists who were tempted to pass through the looking glass into the self-indulgent world of their own creations. If an author becomes a character in his own book, the purpose may be for simple autobiography, or it may be to question the very premise of the created work. In post-modern fiction the latter is more apt to be the case. When the author as character begins to question the nature of his art, the result is often the comic portrait of a writer lost in his own novel. No one has satirized this predicament with more confusion and comedy than Kurt Vonnegut. In his seventh novel, *Breakfast of Champions*, the author not only appears as a character, he also holds conversations with himself:

> "This is a very bad book you're writing," I said to myself. . . .
> "I know," I said.[1]

What are readers supposed to do while the author talks to himself?

Vonnegut was dissatisfied with his brief venture into drama and television in the early '70s because the chances for autobiography were too limited:

> . . . I want to be a character in all of my works. I can do that in print. In a movie, somehow, the author always vanishes. Everything of mine which has been filmed so far has been

one character short, and the character is me.[2]

He therefore returned to writing novels which allowed him more scope for self-revelation and self-parody. *Breakfast of Champions*, largely written by 1971 but not published until 1973, is Vonnegut's first novel for the narcissistic decade. No longer content with the limited autobiographical preface common in his earlier books, Vonnegut now introduces himself as a character to observe and participate in the climax of the novel. Suddenly the author appears wearing dark glasses in the cocktail lounge of the Holiday Inn where he has assembled the chief characters of the novel for their violent interaction.

Vonnegut's appearance in his seventh novel is not just a phenomenon of the decade, it is also a natural step in the evolution of his remarkable career. A few years earlier the dark glasses would have been unnecessary—who would have recognized him? In the middle of the '60s Vonnegut's first four novels and his first collection of stories were all out of print. The majority had been issued in paperback, advertised and packaged as science fiction thrillers, sold in drugstores, and soon forgotten. His publishers had warned him that his own personality was not to appear in the pages of fiction. The same was true for his many short stories written for magazines like *Collier's*, *Cosmopolitan*, and the *Saturday Evening Post*. Vonnegut knew how to manipulate the formulas of popular fiction; his stories produced a steady income during the 1950s; but their appearance in popular magazines precluded any critical attention. The moribund state of the magazines themselves soon confirmed Vonnegut's anonymity. After five novels, dozens of stories, and fifteen years of work as a writer, Vonnegut found himself faced with oblivion. His situation was reminiscent of the career of Herman Melville a century before. If a writer achieves early success with a popular form—Melville with his romances of the South Pacific or Vonnegut with his science fiction— how can he attract a new audience when his craft matures and his metaphysical vision deepens? The skeptical themes and experimental forms of Melville's best novels only found a receptive public decades after his death. Vonnegut was very apprehensive about suffering the same eclipse. The specter of a prolific and misunderstood novelist haunted his imagination in the 1960s. It appeared in his novels as the forlorn, embittered, science fiction writer, Kilgore Trout.

At the nadir of his expectations in 1965 Vonnegut decided upon two strategies that might rescue his career from the fate of his fictional novelist. He decided to separate himself from the label of science fiction, and to promote his own image in the public media as often as possible. Consequently he announced in *The New York Times Book Review*: "I have been a sore-head occupant of a file drawer labeled 'science fiction' . . . and I would like out."[3] He also devoted a considerable time to first-person journalism. Readers of magazines like *Esquire, Life, Playboy,* and *Mademoiselle* were offered Vonnegut's latest opinions on everything from astronauts to mass murderers. Many of his journalistic ventures were designed to impress the public with his image as a social satirist. The saving grace of this journalism is its mocking tone and occasional self-parody. His piece on the Maharishi Mahesh Yogi, for example, is entitled "Yes, We Have No Nirvanas."

Vonnegut in 1965 also began two years in residence at the Writers Workshop at the University of Iowa. This contact with other writers and critics helped to move Vonnegut's art in the direction of autobiography. For the first time he was in daily contact with students and critics who pressed him for explanations about his craft. While such academic debate often paralyzes less experienced writers, it proved to be a significant catalyst for the mature fiction of Vonnegut. When his third novel, *Mother Night,* was reissued in 1966, Vonnegut decided to add an autobiographical preface describing his experience during the bombing of Dresden. Two years later he wrote a personal introduction to his collection of stories, *Welcome to the Monkey House,* in which he explored the relationship of life and art. His next novel was *Slaughterhouse-Five* with its opening chapter in the form of an author's confession. Step by step Vonnegut was moving himself onto the stage of his fiction.

Vonnegut seldom explores a possibility for his art without soon beginning to parody its form. The next step for his progressive revelation of self was therefore the self-mocking portrait of the author as character in *Breakfast of Champions.* By the time this novel appeared in 1973 the author was experiencing all of the pressures of literary success. Although a few good reviews had appeared in the early 1960s by writers as perceptive as Terry Southern, serious critical study of Vonnegut's work had not begun until 1966 with articles by C. D. B. Bryan and Robert Scholes. (Vonnegut and Scholes were friends at the Writers Workshop in Iowa.) Then critical appreciation grew so rapidly that in 1971 a full issue of *Critique: Studies in Modern Fiction* was devoted to analysis of Vonnegut's art. His brief residence among the academics, not to mention his advertisements of himself in popular journals, were beginning to pay remarkable dividends. His long-brooding war novel, *Slaughterhouse-Five*, was welcomed in 1969 by scores of favorable reviews. Vonnegut thus began to enjoy the second audience that Melville had never lived to see. The full emergence of Vonnegut as a literary celebrity in the early 1970s provided him with a new public image just ripe for satire in *Breakfast of Champions*. While he was receiving maximum exposure in the various public media, Vonnegut was also devising new ways of representing himself in fiction.

Vonnegut knew that his first novel of the 1970s would attract considerable publicity. Indeed, three book clubs were waiting to offer it as their featured selection. He also assumed that his new novel would be judged against the achievement of *Slaughterhouse-Five*. So much of Vonnegut's own experience had gone into the writing of *Slaughterhouse-Five* that its audience and author alike must have been wondering what he could do next. The novel that comes after a major achievement has always been a special problem for American writers. After the publication of *Moby-Dick* in 1851, Melville's next and seventh novel was the ill-fated *Pierre*. After the success of *Slaughterhouse-Five* in 1969, Vonnegut was afraid that his next book, also his seventh novel, would disappoint his new audience. For awhile he delayed publication of *Breakfast of Champions*. Moreover, he built a negative critical response into the book itself. Anticipating an audience now ready to chip away at his new fame and fortune, Vonnegut presents a comic image of the author dissatisfied with his own work and then attacked by a ravenous dog at the end of the book. The writer thus appears as a character in his own novel, not merely to conduct a dialogue with himself about the relationship of art and life, but also to deflect the charges of his audience. When the dog at the end of the book springs for the jugular vein of the author, our storyteller makes a comic leap over his rented automobile to safety.

Vonnegut's appearance in *Breakfast of Champions* allows him to satirize the limited prospects of his own free will. Ever since his first novel, *Player Piano*, he has been disturbed by the vision of men turning into machines. The threats of automation are displayed frequently in his stories written during the 1950s, and his satire of men as machines is fairly predictable. In the late 1960s, however, Vonnegut was amazed at what happened when his doctor prescribed a drug to help him cope with chronic depression. "I used to think I was responding to Attica or to the mining of Haiphong," he reported, "but I wasn't. I was obviously responding to internal chemistry. All I had to do was take one of these little pills."[4] When this perception is written into *Breakfast of Champions* the result at first is the familiar view of men as robots: "I tend to think of human beings as huge, rubbery test tubes, too, with chemical reactions seething inside" (4). Thus the behavior of a character like Dwayne Hoover is attributed to "bad chemicals," and his disintegration into madness and violence is routine. But when the author introduces himself as a character in the novel, the subject of free will versus mechanical determination becomes more interesting. Then the creative scope of the author is being challenged by one of his own creations. The result is a comic picture of the author caught in the violence of his own invented world. Initially we see the author as a character pretending to be very calm and detached as he looks through his dark glasses at the action in the cocktail lounge of the Holiday Inn. But when the bad chemicals in Dwayne Hoover boil over, the author as character cannot escape the violence: "Somebody jumped backwards to get out of Dwayne's way. He broke my watch crystal, even though I had created him, and he broke my toe" (282).

The full comedy of the author as hapless victim of his own creation is the scene in which Vonnegut's narrative persona is attacked by the Doberman pinscher. The emergency chemicals of the author begin to flow: "My mind sent a message to my hypothalamus, told it to release the hormone CRF into the short vessels connecting my hypothalamus and my pituitary gland" (296). But the comic result is without precedent in medical history—the testicles of the author retract into his abdominal cavity like the landing gear of an airplane and he flies over the automobile. Vonnegut thus enjoys mocking his own image in the novel while also leaping beyond the limited vision of his own satire of men as machines.

Vonnegut's appearance in his own novel allows him to parody his reputation as a hip philosopher. Even his early books had attracted a cult following eager to find metaphysical speculation. Vonnegut had appealed to this audience by including various fantastic religions such as the Church of God of the Utterly Indifferent in *The Sirens of Titan* or Bokononism in *Cat's Cradle*. Despite the comic thrust of his early metaphysical capers, Vonnegut was aware that some readers and critics were solemly discussing his philosophies. No doubt he found the spectacle amusing. When academic critics began to claim with awe that "Vonnegut is wrestling with nothing less than the cosmological question,"[5] who could blame the novelist for laughing to himself? And he encouraged such nonsense by scattering his views on almost every subject throughout the popular journals. During the late 1960s Vonnegut was almost always available for instant wisdom in press interviews, talk shows, commencement addresses, etc. What his audience didn't always perceive, however, was the amount of self-parody inherent in his public image. He was performing in the spirit of Mark Twain, pretending to be profound, when all along the joke was on the audience. The ironic fruits of this performance were both droll and sobering. His metaphysical comedy bred a solemn debate among critics and disciples about his view of a "meaningful existence," and the debate was often held in a nonsense language. "In the post-apocalyptic void," wrote one frightened critic, "all identity is adventitious."[6] The language of critical discussion thus entered the world of "chrono-synclastic infundibulum" without noticing its own comic echo.

Although he may have enjoyed hearing himself praised as "the foremost serious writer in America today,"[7] Vonnegut was experiencing the bittersweet frustration of being praised for the wrong reasons. When would he be recognized as the foremost comic writer? Vonnegut also began to worry about the critics who were seeing through his parade of metaphysics, observing its shallow absurdity, and yet failing to recognize its comic potential. Leslie Fiedler, for example, was complaining in 1970 that Vonnegut's own "spiritual age is late adolescence." The title of Fiedler's article, "The Divine Stupidity of Kurt Vonnegut," and the fact that it appeared in *Esquire*, the home of some of Vonnegut's own writing, were both disconcerting. But a worse attack was published the next year by Charles Samuels in *The New Republic*. He declared that Vonnegut "can tell us nothing worth knowing except what his rise itself indicates: ours is an age in which adolescent ridicule can become a mode of upward mobility."[8] Samuels at least did not take the metaphysical performance of Vonnegut with great solemnity—"A sententious old salt in ontological drag"—but he still implied that Vonnegut would like his philosophy to be accepted without irony. Nothing could be further from the truth. Vonnegut decided to counter such false impressions by increasing the self-parody in his next novel, *Breakfast of Champions*, and by placing such misunderstandings at the very center of his narrative.

Breakfast of Champions is about a novelist known as Kilgore Trout who is invited to attend an art conference in Midland City. There he meets his potential audience, Dwayne Hoover, who rapidly becomes insane after one reading of a Trout novel. The mad rampage of Hoover who injures eleven people and bites off the end of Trout's finger is a mock description of the conduct of Vonnegut's own audience and its penchant for biting the hand that feeds it.

Kilgore Trout, familiar to readers of earlier Vonnegut novels, achieves a new significance in *Breakfast of Champions*. Although he travels to the art conference in order to reveal the face of failure to a naive and uncomprehending audience, he unexpectedly meets his creator and is granted ironic freedom. It is even reported that Trout will soon receive a Nobel Prize. The public will read his science fiction as if it were true, and he will be awarded the Nobel Prize for medicine! With such bravado Vonnegut is simultaneously mocking the solemn incomprehension of his own audience and exorcising the specter of a failed career. Better the wrong Nobel Prize than none at all! At the end of the novel the persona of the author is introducing himself to his characters:

> "Mr. Trout," I said, "I am a novelist, and I created you
> for use in my books."
> "Pardon me?" he said.
> "I'm your Creator," I said. "You're in the middle of a
> book right now—close to the end of it, actually."
> "Um," he said. (299)

The comic disbelief of a character face to face with his own author completes the irony of Vonnegut's performance.

The appearance of the author's persona in *Breakfast of Champions*, no matter how baffled and foolish and hurt the persona may be, still exposes Vonnegut to the charge of self-indulgence. Trout's fiction is described as "solipsistic whimsy," and the same label has been applied by more than one critic to Vonnegut's novel. The criticism is encouraged by the tone and style of the book which readers often find exasperating and silly. The tone is deliberately simple-minded. The persona of the author is pretending to tell the story as if he were reporting events on a distant and dying planet. The style includes drawings by the author of obvious things such as a light switch, a cow, and a hamburger. "I've often thought," Vonnegut once declared, "there ought to be a manual to hand to little kids, telling them what kind of planet they're on, why they don't fall off it, how much time they've probably got here . . . I tried to write one once. It was called *Welcome to Earth*. But I got stuck on explaining why we don't fall off the planet."[9] *Breakfast of Champions* unfortunately sounds like such a manual, and it is not surprising that so many readers have resented being addressed in such a manner.

The strategy of the novel, however, is less sentimental and patronizing than at first it seems. Vonnegut's satire depends on a perception of the difference between the author and his naive persona. The voice of the author as a character is seldom without irony. Although the persona of the author does conform with some of the known facts of Vonnegut's life—date of birth, details about parents, and concerns about mental health—the persona is an obtuse, comic, self-parody of the novelist.

Vonnegut reveals the identity of the persona very early in the novel:

> What do I myself think of this particular book? I feel lousy about it, but I always feel lousy about my books. My friend Knox Burger said one time that a certain cumbersome novel ". . . read as though it had been written by Philboyd Studge." That's who I think I am when I write what I am seemingly programmed to write. (4)

The same voice says a paragraph later: "I am programmed at fifty to perform childishly." The first person pronoun is prominent, but who is the "I" speaking to us? Vonnegut happens to be fifty at the time, but this preface to the novel is signed by Philboyd Studge. The comic name belongs to the narrator who serves as a self-parody of Vonnegut, but the name comes from a short story by Saki about the perversity of public taste and the ingratitude suffered by a poor artist.[10]

Saki's brief tale, "Filboid Studge, The Story of a Mouse that Helped," tells about an artist who encourages a huge demand for an awful breakfast cereal merely by calling it "Filboid Studge." Vonnegut's *Breakfast of Champions* is not only named after a famous advertising slogan for a breakfast cereal, a registered trademark for

Wheaties, it is also narrated by Philboyd Studge, the name created in Saki's story to sell the most unpalatable breakfast cereal of all time. The poor artist in the story advertises the cereal by picturing a fashionable public in hell where the tempting cereal is just beyond their reach. Filboid Studge is thus the image of what the damned public wants but cannot enjoy, and the artist who gives them the image remains at the end of the story unrewarded. The perversity of public taste and the ingratitude faced by an artist are among the chief themes presented and mocked in Vonnegut's novel. The style and tone are consistent with the comic persona called Philboyd Studge. His are the childish observations about common things. His are the drawings scrawled with a felt-tipped pen. But who wants to read a novel told and illustrated by the namesake of a breakfast cereal? Even if Vonnegut can be successfully separated from Philboyd Studge, the responsibility for creating the self-parody still belongs with the novelist.

What advantages, if any, come from having Philboyd Studge serve as the narrator of *Breakfast of Champions*? If satire depends upon irony, perhaps it is helpful to have a naive storyteller who seems to know less about things than either the author or the audience. This is the familiar strategy of *Gulliver's Travels*, and the adventures of Gulliver are not far removed from the comic accidents of Philboyd Studge. Both serve as first-person narrators telling us about their experiences which neither can fully understand or control. Gulliver's assumed superiority to the King of the Brobdingnagians is just as ironic as the conceit of Philboyd Studge. Gulliver's admiration for the Houyhnhnms is just as ridiculous as the naiveté of Vonnegut's narrator. The misadventures of both storytellers—captured by the Lilliputians or injured at the Holiday Inn—are comic and absurd. The humor comes from our recognition that Lemuel Gulliver and Philboyd Studge, despite their pretensions of superiority, are still quintessential Yahoos. The reputation of Jonathan Swift as the greatest satirist in the English language is commonly accepted even though critics still disagree about how to distinguish Swift and Gulliver and how to interpret Gulliver's final response to the Houyhnhnms. Such critical problems are inherent in satire. Thus it is hardly surprising that contemporary readers have difficulty when it comes to separating Vonnegut from his persona and interpreting the narrator's response. Gulliver's final resentment over the pride of the Yahoos is just as ironic as the last tear shed by Vonnegut's narrator over the fate he cannot understand.

The naive storyteller in *Breakfast of Champions* allows Vonnegut to maintain a point of view that is consistent with his satire. The result is a comic survey of American culture and history. The narrator sounds like an anthropologist telling us about a primitive society on a dying planet. His drawings are presented as evidence of the unbelievable artifacts his research has uncovered. The comedy depends upon our recognition that all of his evidence is absolutely common. In the same manner, what Gulliver discovered in all of his travels was merely an exaggeration of what was observable at home. Although Vonnegut's narrator may brag about his ability to jump over cars and somersault through the void, it is clear at the Holiday Inn that he cannot move fast enough to avoid a broken toe. The comedy of satire depends upon the limitations of the storyteller.

Once the narrator of *Breakfast of Champions* is viewed as a parody of the author, the many conversations in the novel about the very process of writing are understandable in a new context. When the narrator says to himself—"this is a very bad book you're writing"—we should hear the naive despair of Philboyd Studge unable to live up to the standards of the Houyhnhnms. If the dissatisfaction were Vonnegut's, there would be no excuse for publishing the book. But if the feeling belongs to the naive storyteller, then Vonnegut succeeds in mocking the fears and pretensions of his fictional author.

If the result were simply another book which calls attention to its own artifice, the hostile reception it has received would be fully justified. "Who doesn't prefer art," writes John Barth, "that at least overtly imitates something other than its own processes? That doesn't continually proclaim 'Don't forget I'm an artifice!'"[11] But the inclusion of a character in *Breakfast of Champions* who claims to be the author of the book is not merely Vonnegut's way of calling attention to himself in the process of writing, it is also his way of satirizing the contemporary self-conscious novel. Indeed, Vonnegut's book makes fun of the very kind of art that Barth himself often practices. *Breakfast of Champions* is a burlesque of the narcissistic pretensions of the 1970s.

Vonnegut's narrator assumes a self-indulgent tone at the beginning when he announces: "This book is my fiftieth birthday present to myself" (5). The birthday celebration is viewed as a time to take stock of the many characters in the author's head. "I think I am trying to clear my head of all the junk in there . . . I'm throwing out characters from my other books, too. I'm not going to put on any more puppet shows." Vonnegut is mocking that decisive moment in an author's career when he feels ready to abandon his cast of characters. The best examples in English literature are Shakespeare allowing Prospero to dismiss the "elves of hills, brooks, standing lakes and groves" and W. B. Yeats concluding that his circus animals will no longer be on show.

Prospero's words, which echo Medea in Ovid, are both apologetic and proud. Despite his references to "weak masters" and "rough magic," the poetry reverberates with the proud knowledge of his accomplishments. Prospero has imitated the power of the gods—"to the dread rattling thunder/Have I given fire and rifted Jove's stout oak/With his own bolt." Shakespeare is about to retire from the London stage, and it is hardly a time for modesty about his "potent art." Vonnegut, however, has no intentions of ending his career (two more novels will follow *Breakfast of Champions* in the same decade) and the farewell gestures of his comic persona are both vain and disingenuous. Vonnegut's narrator has very limited power to create or destroy. He is trapped and victimized in the world of his own characters. Any attempt to assume godlike power leads quickly to a pratfall. The more he tries to clear his head, the faster the junk inside appears to multiply.

His gesture of dismissal—"I'm not going to put on any more puppet shows"—sounds closer to the disappearing circus animals of Yeats, but Vonnegut's narrator is merely exhibiting a false bravado at age fifty, and not the final realization that old themes and characters can no longer be summoned when it is time to "lie down where all the ladders start,/In the foul rag-and-bone shop of the heart." Vonnegut's naive persona hides behind his dark glasses at the Holiday Inn, and never approaches his own heart. The self-indulgent tone of the narrator celebrating his own birthday, and the self-deluded gesture of dismissing his own characters, indicate the scope of Vonnegut's satire of storytelling in a narcissistic decade.

The full comedy of the author attempting to dismiss his own characters occurs near the end of *Breakfast of Champions*. The author in a rented Plymouth Duster is chasing after his most famous creation: "'Whoa! I'm a friend!' I said . . . 'Mr. Trout,' I said from the unlighted interior of the car, 'you have nothing to fear. I bring you tidings of great joy'" (298). The divine pretensions of the author are immediately mocked when he attempts to turn on the light and merely succeeds in activating the windshield wipers. When it comes to the climactic moment of freeing his character he invokes the memory of Count Tolstoi freeing his serfs and Thomas Jefferson freeing his slaves, but the great emancipation ironically backfires. When the author says, "Arise, Mr. Trout, you are free, you are *free*," the character suddenly appears to have the face of the author's father, and his last words are: "Make me young, make me young, make me young!" The result of bringing the comic author face to face with the image of his own father is to undercut his pride as a creator. He has no more power to set his creation free than he does to make his father young. Indeed, if the character is the father of the author, then the very tables of creation have been turned. Vonnegut, of course, is the father of both the character and the comic author, and the disillusionment of both in the novel completes Vonnegut's self-parody and his satire of the vain delusions of narcissistic authors.

If the chief delusion of an author is the attempt to assume divine creative power, Vonnegut deliberately mocks his comic persona for indulging such pretensions. We should laugh at the vanity of the narrator when he modestly announces: "I was on a par with the Creator of the Universe there in the dark in the cocktail lounge" (205). We might also recall that the same narrator has been complaining about the incompetence, the cruelty, and the indifference of the Creator at frequent intervals throughout the novel. He has often referred to a God who moves in disastrous ways creating tornadoes and tidal waves or destroying a whole galaxy for the mere pleasure of the fireworks. Thus when the narrator introduces himself as being "on a par with the Creator," he is vainly assuming some rather dubious credentials.

The dialogue between the comic author and the bewildered Kilgore Trout is a wonderful example of baffled condescension and suspicious distrust. The author playing God in his rented car has promised "tidings of great joy," but Trout's response to the good news is a noncommittal "Um." Frustrated by the ungrateful response, the author says, "If I were in your spot, I would certainly have lots of questions." Trout's wary reply is: "do you have a gun?" Trout has a good reason to be suspicious of anyone approaching him in a car. Earlier in the novel he was "kidnapped by pure evil in a white Oldsmobile" and left unconscious after losing his money. How can Kilgore

Trout be certain that the author in the rented Plymouth is not a member of the Pluto Gang ready to strike again?

The narrator however wants to bless his creation with the gift of harmony: "'Mr. Trout I love you,' I said gently. 'I have broken your mind to pieces. I want to make it whole. I want you to feel wholeness and inner harmony such as I have never allowed you to feel before'" (300-301). And what does Trout see in the hand of his benevolent creator? An apple! There is no sign at all that Vonnegut's comic author in the role of God recognizes what will come from the fruit he so kindly offers. Unknowingly, he is placing his favorite character in the same position that is described in Trout's novel, *Now It Can Be Told*. This science fiction novel is written in the form of a letter from the Creator of the Universe to "the only creature in the entire Universe who has free will." When this message from the Creator was read by Dwayne Hoover, who was just insane enough to believe it, the result was his mad rampage through the Holiday Inn. When the apple of freedom is offered to Kilgore Trout by his naive creator, who believes the apple is "a symbol of wholeness and harmony and nourishment," the poor science fiction writer thinks his creator is merely playing one final joke upon him. The offer of freedom is therefore met with the desperate wish that all of the knowledge and experience of the tempting fruit could be withdrawn—"Make me young, make me young, make me young!"

Vonnegut, of course, is the creator of the comic author, who in turn plays God and pretends to be the creator of Kilgore Trout, who in turn is the author of *Now It Can Be Told* which describes the Creator of the Universe making the promise of free will. "My books," Vonnegut has said, "are essentially mosaics made up of a whole bunch of little chips; and each chip is a joke."[12] The humor reflects on all of the authors in and out of Vonnegut's book who assume the guise of divine power only to discover the knowledge of evil that comes from their best intentions. The last joke is on author and characters alike—the tidings of great joy become paradise lost.

Notes

[1] Kurt Vonnegut, Jr., *Breakfast of Champions* (New York: Delacorte Press, 1973), p.198. All further references to this novel are cited parenthetically.

[2] Kurt Vonnegut, Jr., *Between Time and Timbuktu* (New York: Delacorte Press, 1972), p. xv.

[3] Kurt Vonnegut, Jr., "Science Fiction," *New York Times Book Review*, September 5, 1965, p. 2.

[4] Kurt Vonnegut, Jr., *Wampeters, Foma, and Granfalloons* (New York: Delta, 1975), p. 252.

[5] David H. Goldsmith, *Kurt Vonnegut, Fantasist of Fire and Ice* (Bowling Green: University Popular Press, 1972), p. 10.

[6] Richard Giannone, *Vonnegut, A Preface To His Novels* (New York: Kennikat Press, 1977), p. 61.

[7] Jerome Klinkowitz, *Vonnegut in America* (New York: Delacorte Press, 1977), p. 33.

[8] Charles Samuels, "Age of Vonnegut," *New Republic*, 164 (June 12, 1971), p. 30.

[9] *Wampeters, Foma, and Granfalloons*, p. 276.

[10] Vonnegut's source for his narrator's comic name was first pointed out by Derek Roper at the University of Sheffield.

[11] John Barth, *Lost in the Funhouse* (New York: Bantam, 1969), p. 114.

[12] "*Playboy* Interview," *Playboy*, 20 (July 1973), p. 58.

1974

Toni Morrison
Sula

What was America reading in 1974 while the morality play of Watergate dominated the public media? Several rabbits and one shark were the main characters in the most popular fiction of the year. *Watership Down* and *Jaws* remained on the Bestseller List of *The New York Times* for more than seven months. While the television cameras focused on the self-destruction of the Nixon presidency, the rabbits in Richard Adam's novel were practicing survival. When the news of Watergate began to fade, the popular audience could turn to Peter Benchley's novel to cheer for the shark. It was not a great year for politics or literature.

One hope for American literature was Joseph Heller's long-expected *Something Happened*. After the wit and satire of his first novel, *Catch-22*, the public had been waiting thirteen years for Heller's second book. The advance publicity forced *Something Happened* onto the Bestseller List for awhile, but the public soon could see that almost nothing happens in more than five hundred pages. Its companion in 1974 was James Michener's *Centennial*, another long novel in which everything happens with the speed and significance of cartoon history. For their claims on public attention Heller and Michener ought to be sentenced to years of hard labor reading one another's novels.

The finest novel of the year could not compete with the rabbits and sharks on the Bestseller List. Nor could its slight volume compare with the monstrous hulks pushed into the marketplace by Heller and Michener. It was written by a woman who was largely unknown, divorced, and black. Toni Morrison's *Sula* did sell approximately 12,000 hardback copies, and it was nominated for the National Book

Award, but in the year of political drama and literary disappointment the public hardly began to realize that American fiction had a new champion.

Morrison was thirty-six when she began writing about the black community of her childhood in the Midwest. Her first novel, *The Bluest Eye* (1970), sold a few thousand copies, and gathered some complimentary reviews. Working as an editor at Random House did not leave Morrison very much time for the writing of her own fiction. Her second novel, *Sula*, was created in part while commuting on the subway to her office in New York. Nevertheless it appears to come intact from that core of imagination where experience, vision, and craft are inseparable.

Sula is less than two hundred pages long, but it does include the drama of a threatened community like *Watership Down*, the promise of sudden violence typical of *Jaws*, the killing of a child in *Something Happened*, and the independence of pioneer women in *Centennial*. Theme and character are held together by a narrative strategy that is both traditional and modern. Morrison begins with a picture of the community and then measures the individuality of her characters against the common judgment. This method is as old as the art of the novel, but Morrison makes it new by separating the narrative into scattered episodes for the reader to assemble. "I thought of *Sula* as a cracked mirror," says the novelist, "fragments and pieces we have to see independently and put together."[1] The image of a cracked mirror is rather familiar in the criticism of postmodern fiction, but Morrison is following the lead of Faulkner and his fragmented narrative vision of the funeral journey in *As I Lay Dying*. Although her novel is told in the third person, the events in *Sula* are often dramatized from the different viewpoints of individual characters. Also in the tradition of Faulkner's novel, one character is insane, a mother commits adultery, and the strongest character, Sula, reports her own death.

The fragments to assemble are scattered over several decades—the chapters have dates which range from 1919 to 1965—and the points of view include the mad, dying, and righteous. The narrative focus is largely shared by two women who are girlhood friends. "I have written *Sula*," Morrison admits, "to talk about something I had known—about friendship in the fullest sense as it existed for certain black women and other immigrant or pioneering types—women who, because of their race and sex, were dependent on each other sometimes literally for their very survival. . . . In *Sula*, I wanted to portray such a friendship as a valid experience."[2] The boldness of the subject matter will seem more apparent if it is recalled that James Baldwin could still refer a few years before to the "as yet unwritten history of the Negro woman."

Four generations of black women are dramatized in Morrison's book, but the focus largely remains on the two girlhood friends. Nel Wright is sheltered by very conservative parents who find comfort in the respectability of home and church. The fear and self-denial that hide behind the pose of respectability are first glimpsed when Nel and her mother travel to New Orleans. The little girl sees her mother humiliated by the train conductor, and she thereupon resolves to "be on guard—always."

Nel's only chance for self-discovery comes with the friendship of Sula who is inherently strong-willed and independent. Sula's one-legged grandmother killed her only son, catapulted herself through an upstairs window, and still is alive decades later at the end of the novel. Sula's mother enjoyed sex with every man in the neighborhood, but only during the day, because she felt that spending the night with someone implied a "definite commitment." Sula inherits the strength to inflict pain—even as a child she cuts off the end of a finger to warn the local boys—and she grows up to think of sex as "pleasant and frequent, but otherwise unremarkable."[3]

Nel and Sula are partners in nearly everything, including the murder of a small child, but when Nel is conventional enough to marry, Sula thinks nothing of breaking the marriage with adultery. The spectacle of Nel playing the role of wronged wife then convinces Sula that her friend, after all, "belonged to the town and all of its ways" (120). Sula meets an early death, and Nel waits more than twenty-five years before understanding the sorrow and loss of her friend, partner, and other self.

The narrator of *Surfacing* may explore the depths of her own psyche, but the other characters in Atwood's novel are merely her satellites. Morrison, however, can fully explore what her characters mean to one another because her narrative method is not limited to one point of view. When the fragments of time and character are put together, the result is a full drama of friendship and betrayal.

The individuals in Morrison's fiction appear fully defined because they live in a community prepared to measure their conduct.

Sula's neighbors, for example, watch her behavior, and conclude that she is a genuine agent of the devil. The conflict between the standards of a community and the freedom of an individual can be traced from the very beginning of the American imagination. The first Puritans in the Massachusetts Bay Colony were famous for declaring one another heretics, and a few of the more outspoken individuals were exiled to the wilderness of Rhode Island. Two hundred years later the tension of conformity and individualism remains the central theme of Hawthorne, Twain, etc. Novelists in the twentieth century, however, have found it more difficult to suggest any convincing sense of a community against which individual conduct can be measured. If a protagonist feels resigned to the "benign indifference of the universe" his individual conduct is not important.

The conviction that nothing matters is the problem that so many contemporary writers have had to confront. Bellow shows the random violence of urban life in *Mr. Sammler's Planet*, but his one-eyed philosopher can do little more than lament the decline and fall of western civilization. Updike presents the suburban view in *Rabbit Redux* where the merest hint of individuality is destroyed—Jill is burned, Skeeter is banished—to allow the community to remain faceless. Atwood takes the narrator of *Surfacing* into a wilderness of nature and mind where neither freedom nor conformity have any traditional meaning. Vonnegut in *Breakfast of Champions* can only parody the dilemma of the narrator who believes that an individual writer can speak for a community.

Morrison is the exception among contemporary novelists because she appears almost totally immune to the dominant myth of our century—meaninglessness. Although she knows that "to mean anything is not in vogue," she believes that "narrative remains the best way to learn anything," and therefore "I continue with narrative form."[4] She can make sense out of individual conduct because her vision of the community is intact. "After my first novel, *The Bluest Eye*, writing became a way to be coherent in the world. It became necessary and possible for me to sort out the past."[5] Morrison has little patience with the fashions of incoherence—what Marjorie Perloff calls the "poetics of indeterminacy"—because the aim of her narrative includes the satisfaction of making sense. "My genuine criticism of most contemporary books," complains Morrison, "is that they're not *about* anything."

How can she escape the modern condition of anonymity and aimlessness? Doesn't she live in New York City like Mr. Sammler? Doesn't she feel the boredom of contemporary America like Harry Angstrom? Doesn't she look for herself at the expense of others like Atwood's narrator? Doesn't she share the irony of Vonnegut's situation? Not exactly. Morrison is different because she is black, and she has something to write about because she can recall the stories and characters of a special community. "I write what I have recently begun to call village literature, fiction that is really for the village, for the tribe." Morrison wants to be viewed as a black writer—her subject she claims has "its peculiar brand of irony, oppression, versatility, madness, joy, strength, shame, honor, triumph, grace, and stillness"—but the important requirement for her art is the coherent vision of a community.[6] It is the sort of vision that enabled Faulkner to give narrative form to the history and legend of his native Mississippi, and perhaps the kind of vision that allows Isaac Bashevis Singer to find the coherence in his stories about Poland. In each case the writer is able to work closely with a folk tradition, identify with the history of a people, and create the narrative of a community that is threatened or doomed.

"In that place," Morrison begins *Sula*, "there was once a neighborhood." The place still exists in the memory of the narrator even though the neighborhood in fact has been replaced by suburbs. "Everything I write starts there," admits Morrison, "it's my beginning ... I have done whatever it is that writers do to places, and made it my own."[7] The setting of her first novel is identified as Lorain, Ohio, where Morrison herself was raised. The town in *Sula* is named "Medalion," but the closeness of fiction and reality is clear. In her third and fourth novels the settings range further away, but the vision of community is still intact with the hometowns of the characters Milkman and Son.

The first pages of *Sula* identify the setting, relate its history—how the black community on the hill came to be known as the Bottom—and indicate its doomed future. By telling us at the beginning that soon "there will be nothing left of the Bottom," Morrison sets up her novel as a series of flashbacks. The effect is to draw the reader back into a time and community that are lost. "The village participates in the story," explains Morrison, "the narrator functions as chorus."[8] If this narrative strategy is to be successful, the community must be rendered with specific detail. When the narrator thinks of the coming destruction of Reba's Grill, she doesn't forget the owner who "cooked in her hat because she couldn't remember the ingredients without it."

The tone of the narrative can be comic and tragic at the same time. Even at the brightest moments we are reminded that the neighborhood on the hill is called the Bottom. "I'm trying to do what I call a Black style," says Morrison, "Not *the* Black style, but *a* Black style."[9] She explains how it is held together by "a spine that's very biblical and meandering and aural—you really have to hear it." Reading any novel by Morrison is like listening to the thoughts and conversation of a village: sad, comic, wise, and haunted by dreams, fear, and death. "Peasants don't write novels," says Morrison, "because they don't need them. They have a portrait of themselves from gossip, tales, music, and some celebrations."[10] When the village life disappears, however, the world is lucky to have the imaginative recall of Toni Morrison. While commuting to her office in Manhattan, she can recreate the "gossip, tales, music, and some celebrations" of the lost community. Thus another place like Faulkner's Yoknapatawpha County is added to the map of literature.

After the sense of place has been established, the community may begin to observe the conduct of a few individuals. Morrison therefore reports near the end of the first chapter that the people up in the Bottom are "preoccupied with earthly things—and each other, wondering even as early as 1920 what Shadrack was all about, what that little girl Sula who grew into a woman in their town was all about..." (5-6). The novel which really begins on the next page is the sum of all those wonderings. The two characters who cause the most speculation, Shadrack and Sula, are the most extraordinary individuals. They live alone: Shadrack with his insanity, Sula with her selfishness. He only speaks one word to her in the whole novel, but that word is "always." Perhaps the community is right to view them both as agents of the devil.

Morrison has a special talent for describing eccentric characters, and Shadrack is among her very best. He is "blasted and permanently astonished" by his first experience with war on a French battlefield in 1917. Never fully regaining his sanity, he finds a marginal existence as fisherman and drunkard for the neighborhood of Bottom. He thus joins a gallery of characters who live on the fringe of Morrison's fictional community: the splendid whore known as Maginot Line in *The Bluest Eye*, the woman in *Song of Solomon* who keeps her father's bones hanging in a sack in the living room, and the nearly blind Thérèse in *Tar Baby* who brings the hero at the end to his supernatural fate.

The madness of Shadrack, of course, makes a lot of sense. He is the founder of National Suicide Day because he reasons that if one day a year is devoted to the celebration of sudden death, then the rest of the year will be safe. His celebration harmlessly becomes a part of the calendar of Bottom until one year half the neighborhood follows him to a tunnel being built under the river. Several people die when the tunnel suddenly collapses. Morrison presents this drama in less than a page of economy, detail, precision, and horror. Nothing in the great volume of Michener's *Centennial* or Heller's *Something Happened* is nearly as effective. Shadrack himself doesn't enter the tunnel: "Having forgotten his song and his rope, he just stood there high up on the bank ringing, ringing his bell" (162). He remains a sympathetic character because we know the origin of his mental condition and we know it was not his intention for people to die in the tunnel.

A lesser novelist might not bother to explain the history of the town lunatic, but it is typical of Morrison to render a full account. In her first novel there is a minor eccentric, Soaphead Church, who is a "Reader, Adviser, & Interpreter of Dreams." Although his role in the novel is small, Morrison quickly traces his family back to the early 1800s. She is not interested in detail for the sake of detail; she wants to "sort out the part" because it is the way "to be coherent in the world." The history of Shadrack is therefore important for an understanding of the complete picture. He may seem to have little or nothing to do with the normal life of the community. Like his namesake in the Bible, he is not much interested in the worship of golden idols. No one except Sula ever visits his shack by the river which he keeps neat and clean with the habit of military discipline. Shadrack nevertheless is saved by his creator for the last page of the novel where he and Nel move "in opposite directions, each thinking separate thoughts about the past." He has survived most of the community that once tried to measure his individuality. Sula's old friend is left to mourn the destruction of the neighborhood, and Shadrack is still moving the other way.

Shadrack and Sula are both outcasts, but Morrison shows how different the world looks from each point of view. After the identity of Shadrack is blasted away in the war, he is too frightened "to acknowledge the fact that he didn't even know who or what he was ... no part, no language, no tribe ... nothing nothing nothing to do" (12). At the heart of his madness there is fear and emptiness, and he is condemned to the margin of the community because his identity is essentially missing. Sula, however, gradually discovers that she cannot trust the judgment of others, and thus her only choice is self-reliance. She leaves the community entirely for ten years, and only comes back after deciding that self-imposed exile is no better than being an outcast at home.

Two events in her childhood cause her to question the normal bonds of the community. The first seems trivial but is never forgotten. By accident she overhears her mother express a dislike for children. If her mother is capable of such betrayal, the young girl concludes "there was no other that you could count on" (118). The second event is much worse. Sula is teasing a younger child named Chicken Little. He slips from her hands while being swung around in the air, sails into the river, and sinks to his death. Sula and Nel both watch helplessly as the water "closed quickly over the place where Chicken Little sank" (61). This experience teaches her that she cannot even trust herself to obey the most basic law of the community—"Thou shalt not kill." When her mother accidently burns to death, Sula watches the fire with the interest of a connoisseur. When her grandmother turns an only son into a kerosene torch, Sula is suitably impressed. It should come as no surprise that Sula herself never marries or has children. Her life is spent "exploring her own thoughts and emotions, giving them full reign, feeling no obligation ... hers was an experimental life" (118).

Ten years of college and travel away from Medalion do not change Sula. The men in cities from Nashville to San Diego are all the same—"a lover was not a comrade and could never be" (121). Sula would like to find "the other half of her equation," but the quest is in vain. Atwood's narrator in *Surfacing* anticipates wholeness beyond the struggle with the images of death, but Sula cannot forget the sight of her mother burning or the water closing over the head of Chicken Little. Sula is lacking a coherent self—"no center ... around which to grow"—and that is why no one can ever be that "version of herself which she sought to reach out to." Sula has intelligence, strength, wit, courage, passion, charm, and gaity, but she is doomed to be the loneliest character in contemporary literature. Her many sexual adventures merely reinforce "a loneliness so profound the word itself had no meaning" (123). The men are interchangeable and anonymous because "the solitude she found in that desperate terrain had never admitted the possibility of other people." The one man who begins to fill the emptiness typically makes his exit before Sula realizes that she doesn't even know his name.

The antipathy of the community for Sula increases when they believe that she is guilty of "the unforgivable thing"—sleeping with white men. The charge may or may not be true, but in any case the loneliness she feels is determined more by private failure than public censure. Her identity is not threatened by the sort of racial prejudice experienced by the hero of Ellison's *Invisible Man*. He is misunderstood and made invisible by a white community which is blinded by racial stereotypes. Sula is also misunderstood and subject to extraordinary loneliness, but it is the black community which casts her out because they think she is a devil. The hero of Ellison's novel finds his solitude after stripping away all of his illusions, hopes, and ideals. Sula doesn't have any to begin with, except the one ideal of friendship based on her experience with Nel, and that is destroyed when Nel marries. After the hero of *Invisible Man* is taken apart piece by piece, neither Ellison nor any other writer has been able to put him together again. Morrison has another goal. She has created one of the most remarkable images of a black woman in American literature by going beyond racial concerns to show the tragic solitude that any soul may inherit.

The scene in which the good ladies of the community decide that Sula is a devil is one of the comic highlights of the novel. Their evidence includes several omens, but the conclusive sign is that Shadrack was observed tipping his hat to Sula. The conversation of the ladies is a prologue to a game of cards in Medalion, but it could be a trial conducted in Salem. Sula is not openly persecuted, however, because the black community is prepared to tolerate and survive any disaster—natural or supernatural. Indeed, the return of Sula has several unexpected dividends for the residents of the Bottom. Morrison is very good at showing how the community and the individual influence one another. While the gossip of the town molds Sula as a devil and a pariah, her scornful conduct forces the community to be more virtuous. The women, for example, begin to care more for their men after Sula has rejected them. A mother who spends most of her time at the pool hall suddenly becomes protective and caring after

Sula crosses the path of her child. Having a devil in their midst proves to be a godsend. "They began to cherish their husbands and wives, protect their children, repair their homes and in general band together . . ." (117).

The community is released from its virtue by the early death of Sula. Most of her neighbors are afraid to cross the threshold of a dying witch, but Sula is visited on her deathbed by her girlhood friend. Nel can neither understand nor forgive, but Sula at least has one last chance to ask about the conventions of good and evil—"How you know?" The death of Sula is received as good news by the community, but without her presence their conduct soon reverts to carelessness. Winter comes early to the Bottom, and with the first thaw several of the celebrating townspeople die in the collapsing tunnel.

Morrison is often asked why her novels include so much violence and death. She replies with a smile: "My inclination is in the tragic direction. Maybe it's a consequence of my being a classics minor."[11] The smile is for the naiveté of the audience wanting to know the source of literature. Morrison knows that her characters and stories come from experience, the resources of "inclination," and that her art is shaped by conventions of literature as old as Biblical legend and Greek drama. Even the names in her fiction—Shadrack, Pilate, Solomon, Valerian—are charged with history and myth. Morrison has the best of both worlds—the study and teaching of literature at Howard, Cornell, and Yale, along with the vital memory of a village culture. The violence and death in her fiction are as new as current events (National Suicide Day was invented for *Sula* just a few years before Jonestown) and as old as Greek or Biblical tragedy.

Morrison is also fortunate to be an editor for Random House. The manuscripts of persons as diverse as Muhammad Ali and Angela Davis come across her desk. She has a chance to see in every stage of expression the stories being told, hopes projected, and history discovered. Andrew Young claims that Morrison "has done more to encourage and publish other black writers than anyone I know."[12] Her role in the business of publishing gives Morrison a view of the whole enterprise from early drafts to finished book. When asked to address the American Writers Congress she can speak with authority as an author, teacher, and publisher. Her chief complaint to a recent Congress was aimed at the practice of literary criticism. "Whole schools of criticism," Morrison asserts, "have dispossessed the writer of any place whatever in the critical value of his work."[13] She is disturbed by criticism that follows "postmodern fiction into self-consciousness, talking about itself as though it were the work of art."[14] It is typical of Morrison as author, teacher, and publisher to demand that critical attention be focused directly on "the craft, vision, and meaning" of the work of art.

Since the publication of *Sula* in 1974 Morrison has been in constant demand for interviews, statements, and public appearances. All of the publicity neither distracts her from the serious pursuit of her art—four novels in less than a dozen years—nor distorts her commitment to the multiple and growing audience. As an editor, teacher, and public speaker, Morrison does what she can to educate her audience, help other writers, and promote the value of literature. All of which is possible because as a black woman novelist Morrison has created a fictional world of the first importance. Sula is finally a tragic character because her "curiosity and her gift for metaphor" cannot be expressed—she is an "artist with no art form" (121). Morrison herself has found the form, shaped the voices of memory and imagination into a novel, and thereby added to American fiction one of the most significant tragic heroines since the appearance of Hester Prynne on the scaffold.

Notes

[1] *The New Republic*, 21 March 1981, p. 28.

[2] "Toni Morrison," *Vogue*, 171 (April 1981), 330-331.

[3] Toni Morrison, *Sula* (New York: Alfred A. Knopf, 1974), p. 44. All subsequent references to this novel are cited parenthetically.

[4] *The New Republic*, 21 March 1981, p. 27.

[5] *Ibid.*, p. 25.

[6] *New York Times Magazine*, 11 August 1974, p. 16.

[7] *New York Times Magazine*, 20 May 1979, p. 58.

[8] "A Conversation with Toni Morrison," *Essence*, 12, No. 3 (July 1981), p. 86.

Her comments refer to *Tar Baby*, but are even more applicable to *Sula*.

[9] *Ibid.*, p. 133.

[10] *The New Republic*, 21 March 1981, p. 26.

[11] *Ibid.*, p. 28.

[12] *Newsweek*, 30 March 1981, p. 5..

[13] *The Nation*, 24 October 1981, p. 397.

[14] *The New Republic*, 21 March 1981, p. 29.

1975

E. L. Doctorow
Ragtime

A chorus of praise greeted the publication of E. L. Doctorow's *Ragtime* in the summer of 1975:

> "No recent novelist has brought such possibilities together in a big popular book" (*Newsweek*, 14 July 1975).

> "A unique and beautiful work of art... Doctorow has added a grace to our history" (*Saturday Review*, 26 July 1975).

> "Will be the most read, the most critically applauded, and yes, perhaps the most accoladed novel of the year" (*The New Republic*, 5 July 1975).

With so much attention the novel climbed quickly to the top of the bestseller lists and stayed there for several weeks. More than three million copies of *Ragtime* were soon in print. The advertising campaign was staged with unusual care by Random House. A special edition of the novel had been printed early and distributed to Doctorow's friends and selected media representatives. Doctorow's years in publishing—senior editor for New American Library and editor-in-chief for Dial Press—no doubt helped to make the appearance of *Ragtime* the publishing event of the year.

The successful wave of publicity led within six months to a riptide of criticism. Early in 1976 the reviews began to turn hostile:

> "A simple-minded, whimsical, socio-historical pageant... comes nearer to qualifying as a comic-book" (*Times*

Literary Supplement, 23 January 1976).

"Too much attention on the reader's part kills it stone-
dead" (*Encounter*, February 1976).

"*Ragtime* gets my vote as The Most Overrated Book of
the Year" (*Atlantic Monthly*, January 1976).

Do these negative views represent a sober reconsideration of the value
of the novel, or do they merely indicate annoyance with the uncritical
praise that accompanied the book's appearance? Seldom has a novel
been so well received, then so violently attacked, and all the time so
little understood. While celebrating the dynamic quality of the
narrative, the reviewers did not begin to inquire about the identity of
the narrator. While attacking the mixture of fiction and history, the
critics failed to understand how the two fit together. Why should
Henry Ford, J. P. Morgan, Emma Goldman, Commander Peary,
Sigmund Freud, and Henry Houdini, not to mention two invented
families with opposite backgrounds, all be in the same novel? Neither
praising *Ragtime* as an "inventive mixture of history and fancy," nor
dismissing it as a comic-book, begins to explain its complex design.

"When critics disagree," as Wilde suggested, "the artist is in
accord with himself." Doctorow wisely has accepted his new status as
a literary celebrity without volunteering much comment on the subtlety of his own work. If he is asked to distinguish the fictional and
historical characters, Doctorow replies, "I used to know but I've
forgotten."[1] When asked what liberties have been taken with history,
Doctorow calls his book "a novelist's revenge on an age that celebrates
nonfiction." Three million readers have been left to discover for
themselves the enigmatic nature of the narrator, the significance of
mixing fiction and history, and the double theme of disintegration and
renewal.

Although the novel has been praised and condemned for many
of the wrong reasons, *Ragtime* is a critical as well as a popular step
forward in Doctorow's career. His first novel, *Welcome to Hard Times*,
appeared and disappeared in the early 1960s. About fear, courage,
and violence in the old Dakota Territory, *Welcome to Hard Times* was
turned in to a forgettable western film. His second novel, *The Book of
Daniel*, appeared in 1971, and the praise of a fellow novelist helped
Doctorow to win a nomination for the National Book Award. "A

nearly perfect work of art, a cause for rejoicing," wrote Joyce Carol Oates, "I can think of no higher praise for a work of fiction." *The Book of Daniel* still escaped popular success, but the good reviews and the nomination for the National Book Award set the stage for the commercial breakthrough Doctorow was able to achieve with *Ragtime*.

The complexity of Doctorow's earlier novels should have alerted reviewers to the potential subtlety of *Ragtime*. Doctorow is not an artist content with offering the mere illusion of history. The story of the rise and fall of a western town is told in *Welcome to Hard Times* by a narrator who is a survivor of the history he has suffered, promoted, and perhaps invented. The story of the trial and conviction of the Rosenbergs is transformed in *The Book of Daniel* into a novel with a double narrative structure and a subtle political spectrum. Doctorow ranks high among recent authors—Barth, Pynchon, Vonnegut—willing to experiment with the form of the novel in order to reach an artful compromise with modern history. The wide popularity of *Ragtime* does not mean that Doctorow has abandoned his experimental approach to the form of the novel or departed from the quality of his earlier work. The structure of *Ragtime* is complex and intricate, but the surface of the novel is so rich with events and personalities that its dynamic life may be quickly enjoyed without pausing to analyze its remarkable design. Thus the great popularity of the book, and the equally great incomprehension.

The first problem is to locate the narrator. Almost all of the fictional characters belong to two families: one in New Rochelle with a prosperous father who sells flags and fireworks, and a poor immigrant family in New York with a father who makes silhouettes. Before the novel is over the families will merge and their fortunes will reverse. The narrator of the novel refers to the parents of the New Rochelle family as Father and Mother. Their only child is a little boy who is seen infrequently in the book and seldom appears to be a significant character. A casual reader of the novel might not identify the little boy as the narrator, but enough is gradually revealed about his personality to allow us to see how the novel has been put together from his recollections and his research.

Doctorow does let us know just a few pages into the book that the little boy "had reached that age of knowledge and wisdom in a child when it is not expected by the adults around him and consequently goes unrecognized." Is this the "wisdom and knowledge" necessary to tell the story of his family? If the child is the narrator why does he refer to his parents as Father and Mother but always to himself in the third person as "the little boy"? A similar narrative strategy was used by Doctorow in *The Book of Daniel*, where parts of the story are told by a small boy in the first person, and parts are told by the same character in later years when he looks back upon his childhood and then refers to himself in the third person. But in *Ragtime* the mature or present narrator is never directly introduced. Instead, it is necessary to infer that the little boy has the ability at a later date to look back and assemble the various pieces of his history. At the beginning of the novel it is revealed that the boy reads the newspaper daily and has an enormous interest in the career of Harry Houdini. *Ragtime* often reflects the headline news from 1906 to 1914, and Houdini is a principal character in the novel. The little boy who is fascinated by the career of illusion and escape will later assemble the house of mirrors that is the narrative design of *Ragtime*.

Doctorow waits until Chapter Fifteen to reveal the qualities of the boy's mind and personality which allow him to assemble and focus the events of the novel. Only then does Doctorow explain how the boy "treasured anything discarded. He took his education peculiarly and lived an entirely secret intellectual life."[2] The novel is an extraordinary montage of bits and pieces discarded from the past, and it is the secret intellectual life of the little boy which causes the many images to be saved and put together. The journal of a trip to the North Pole recorded by his father and the artistic silhouettes cut by his stepfather both eventually come into the possession of the little boy. Thus he gains the evidence necessary to tell about the journey to the Arctic with Commander Peary and to imagine the frustration of the immigrant artist cutting silhouettes on a street corner in New York.

If gathering scraps from the past is the secret activity of the little boy, what sense of order will he be able to impose upon them? "He was alert not only to discarded materials," Doctorow says of his narrator, "but to unexpected events and coincidences." Few novels since Dickens have possessed so many unexpected events and coincidences. Freud and Jung sail through the Tunnel of Love together on their 1909 visit to Coney Island. J. P. Morgan emerges from the Great Pyramid at Giza just in time to see the New York Giants swarming over the Sphinx. Harry Houdini is hanging upside down over Times Square when he recalls, too late, how he might have saved the life of

Archduke Ferdinand. *Ragtime* is a comic novel, and much of the comedy depends upon the coincidences of history and fiction that come together in the mind of the narrator.

What education does the narrator have to enable him to assemble the comic patterns? "He learned nothing at school," it is reported, "so it was left to Grandfather to cultivate what might be the boy's oddity or merely his independence of spirit." Grandfather is a retired professor of classics, and he tells the boy stories from Ovid. "They were stories of people who became animals or trees or statues. They were stories of transformation." With this education it is not surprising that the little boy becomes the narrator of a novel about transformations. He will describe how his own father is transformed from a confident explorer into a frustrated and helpless man. When this parent is lost with the sinking of the Lusitania, the little boy will acquire a new father who has experienced an even more remarkable transformation—from an immigrant Latvian socialist to a successful Hollywood producer. While some of the historical figures in the book, J. P. Morgan and Henry Ford, discuss their belief in reincarnation, the fictional characters are shown in the stages of their metamorphoses. The narrator's uncle will change from a secret admirer of Evelyn Nesbit to a secret agent of protest and revolution. Coalhouse Walker will change from a ragtime piano player to a violent terrorist who threatens to destroy the Morgan Library. The most accomplished performer of quick changes of course is Houdini who has long been the little boy's idol.

The narrator of *Ragtime* listens to his grandfather tell the stories of Ovid, and thereby comes to accept change as the basic condition of life: "Grandfather's stories proposed to him that the forms of life were volatile and that everything in the world could as easily be something else. . . . He found proof in his own experience of the instability of both things and people" (97). This philosophy is suitable for a narrator who must dramatize the flux of American history in the decade prior to World War I. The narrator describes how his own father symbolically shifts from the manufacture of flags and fireworks to military weapons and ammunition. The explosion is more violent than expected when the Lusitania is hit by a German torpedo because the ship is carrying the munitions the narrator's father is supplying to England. If the world in *Ragtime* is drifting into war, the narrator dramatizes the tide of change by selecting the news events from the period which prove "that the forms of life were volatile." The common denominator of such events is violence: the murder of Stanford White, the assassination of Archduke Ferdinand, the vengeance and death of Coalhouse Walker, and the sinking of the Lusitania. The little boy will survive this decade of flux, and later assemble the shifting images in accord with the truth learned from his grandfather about "the instability of both things and people."

The dramatic change in America in the decade prior to World War I is symbolized in the novel by the change of fathers experienced by the narrator. The father who accompanies Commander Peary on his expedition to the North Pole believes at first that all the world exists for him to explore. The flags and fireworks made in his factory contribute to the display of national pride inspired by the administration of Teddy Roosevelt. But just as the blind patriotism of Roosevelt proves inadequate to control either his own political party or his country, the aggressive confidence of the narrator's original father will turn to frustration and defeat. When members of his own family become involved in murder and revolution, the father simply does not know why the world is drifting into violence. His inability to look ahead is dramatically symbolized by his passage on the Lusitania.

The narrator's stepfather will be the immigrant socialist who has risen from poverty as an artist in New York to affluence and power as a filmmaker in Hollywood. The shift in American society suggested by the exchange of fathers is foreshadowed early in the novel by the passing of ships at sea. When the original father sails for the North Pole, he passes a ship full of immigrants just approaching the New World. He has no way of knowing that on that very ship may be the man who will replace him in his own home. The narrator, however, reports that the sight of the immigrant ship is a moment of fear and premonition for his father: "A weird despair seized him."

After some bitter days as an artist in New York, and a troubled period in the textile mills of Massachusetts, the immigrant father follows the example of Benjamin Franklin and finds a new life in Philadelphia. He arrives in Philadelphia with only a few coins, purchases a roll to eat, and like Franklin spends his first day walking the streets of the city. Doctorow's narrator, who loves "unexpected events and coincidences," calls attention to the historical parallel by having the father come by accident to the Franklin Novelty Company where he is soon employed to draw picture books which create the illusion of motion. His work with silhouettes will thus lead to moving pictures.

The success of the immigrant father depends on the extraordinary development of the motion picture industry at the beginning of the century. The first public exhibition of motion pictures on a screen in the United States was presented by Thomas Edison in 1896. Ten years later there were already more than five thousand small theaters, mostly converted stores, showing motion pictures. The making of films in Hollywood began in 1907, and thus the narrator's stepfather will start making pictures in California at the most opportune time. His success is guaranteed because his life is directed "along the lines of flow of American energy."

Does the novel have a character who spends as much time as possible in moving picture theaters? The narrator is identified as one who "liked to go to the moving picture shows downtown," and he is especially fascinated by the metaphysical nature of the images and shadows recorded with the mind's eye. "He knew the principles of photography but saw also that moving pictures depended on the capacity of humans, animals or objects to forfeit portions of themselves, residues of shadow and light which they left behind" (97-98). *Ragtime* is a montage of the shadows and lights accumulated by the little boy who watches all the pictures move and then becomes the narrator of the novel.

The little boy observes the changing of all things, but he is most observant when the image is his own reflection. At the end of the first chapter the boy has a chance to meet Harry Houdini. The magician unexpectedly pays a visit to the boy's family, and parks his touring car in front of their house. What does the little boy do? Characteristically he is preoccupied with "gazing at the distorted macrocephalic image of himself in the shiny brass fitting of the headlight." His world as narrator of *Ragtime* will be a series of comic mirrors.

Chapter Fifteen includes a further analysis of the boy's fascination with reflected images. Doctorow moves beyond the obvious— "and then he took to studying himself in the mirror, perhaps expecting some change to take place before his eyes"—to explore the metaphysics of mirror images:

> He would gaze at himself until there were two selves facing one another, neither of which could claim to be the real one.

> The sensation was of being disembodied. He was no
> longer anything exact as a person. He had the dizzying
> feeling of separating from himself endlessly. (98)

It is the narrator's experience of separation that explains why he refers
to himself in the third person throughout the novel. If the narrator
himself feels the "sensation of being disembodied," it is not surprising
that the reader of the novel may forget how the narrator is related to
the character of the little boy. Few novels have ever been told by a
narrator who thinks of himself as gazing into a mirror and does not
know which image is the real one. Doctorow is able to dramatize a
world of shifting images precisely because his narrator feels that he is
"no longer anything exact as a person." The spectrum of the novel is
produced by the diffraction of the narrator's personality in the mirror
of history.

The importance of mirrors in Doctorow's novels suggests how
much *Ragtime* has in common with the legend of Narcissus. Does the
narrator lose himself like the hero of the Greek myth in the vain
pursuit of his own image? Is the novel a reflection of Shakespeare's
narcissistic Richard II who breaks the mirror in petulant despair because it shows him his own broken face? As the deposed Richard sees
the glass cracked in a hundred shivers, he cannot avoid the thought of
his coming destruction. "A brittle glory shineth in this face," he cries,
"As brittle as the glory is the face." The narrator of *Ragtime* shows a
variety of faces reflected in a decade of history, and he knows that the
images will be shattered when the decade ends in war. It is not the
vanity of the narcissistic quest that so much concerns Doctorow's
narrator, but rather the diffraction of the image and the inevitable
destruction. Mutability and death haunt the final movements of
Ragtime on the eve of international violence. The narrator does not
love what he sees in the mirror, but he is fascinated with the cycles of
change. "It was evident to him that the world composed and recom-
posed itself constantly in an endless process of dissatisfaction."

Does the unrecognized "knowledge and wisdom" of the little
boy include a foreknowledge of the impending cycle of destruction?
If the narrator is telling his story in retrospect, then of course he enjoys
the perspective gained from experience, recollection, and research.
The narrator, for example, has had time to read his father's North Pole
journal, and he even claims to have gained access to Houdini's

unpublished papers. But early in the novel there is a bizarre moment when the dialogue of the little boy, not the voice of the mature narrator, reveals an accurate and unexpected knowledge of the future. At the end of the first chapter, when Houdini visits the family of the narrator, the little boy tells the magician to "Warn the Duke." The remark does not make sense to anyone present, and the boy runs away. Readers of the novel will also be puzzled because thus far in the book there has not been any mention of a Duke. Only at the end of Chapter Thirteen will Houdini unexpectedly meet the ill-fated heir to the Austro-Hungarian throne. At that time Houdini does not remember his message for the Duke. It is only at the end of the novel when Houdini is hanging upside down eleven stories over Times Square that he remembers the warning of the little boy, and realizes, now that it is too late, that perhaps he had a chance to prevent the assassination and the cycle of destruction that will follow.

Houdini's unexpected vision of the little boy at the climax of the novel is a recollection of the first and only meeting of the magician and the future narrator. How could the boy at the beginning of the book have known enough about the future to be able to advise Houdini to warn the unfortunate Archduke? More than one reviewer of the novel has been disturbed by the boy's foreknowledge of the Duke's fate. "This," complains Martin Green in the *American Scholar*, "is merest whimsy. It cannot serve serious imaginative interests."[3] Such criticism tends to ignore the credentials of the boy as the future narrator of the novel, and also to overlook the importance of the moment for Houdini. After the death of his mother, Houdini has followed a second career of exposing the fraud of spiritualists, soothsayers, and various charlatans with their claims of extrasensory perception and clairvoyance. But when he thinks about the warning of the little boy, Houdini decides that "it was the one genuine mystical experience of his life." His attempt to rediscover the boy, however, is frustrated. Houdini returns a week later to the home of the narrator in New Rochelle only to find that the little boy and his family have disappeared. The narrator is typically lost in the mirror of history, and Houdini is left with his inexplicable memory.

At least Houdini retains the memory of "one genuine mystical experience." The majority of the characters in the novel, whether the reflections of history or fiction, all follow adventures that are frustrating and inconclusive. The unsatisfactory nature of the heroic quest is illustrated in a variety of adventures: Commander Peary takes his expedition in search of the North Pole; J. P. Morgan attempts to contact the ancient gods of Egypt by spending a night in the Great Pyramid; Coalhouse Walker seeks justice through revolutionary violence; Houdini wishes to contact his dead mother; and Emma Goldman wants to break the tyranny of capitalism. What do all of these quests have in common? Why does Doctorow bring them all together in *Ragtime*? Doctorow's novel is a picture of western society moving inevitably to the weapons and death of world conflict. Doctorow shows how the many adventures of human will are frustrated, and how the frustration leads to the violence of war.

At the beginning of the novel the father of the narrator believes in heroic deeds and self-fulfillment. He looks forward to the adventure of accompanying Commander Peary to the North Pole. His belief in a perpetual quest is attributed to the philosophy of William James which he received as a student at Harvard. "Exploration became his passion: he wanted to avoid what the great Dr. James had called the habit of inferiority to the full self" (182). But his role in the expedition to the North Pole is far from successful. The father of the narrator cannot tolerate the extreme cold of the Arctic, and he is among the first to turn back. He returns home changed in appearance and spirit. The man who had gone away "burly and self-confident" came back "gaunt and hunched and bearded." He also returns to discover that his wife has become more independent, and that his family has learned to do without him. Whatever the father does in the rest of the novel will leave him with the feeling that the world is slipping away from his control. When he takes his son to a baseball game in New York, all of the players turn out to be rude immigrants, and the father sadly reminds himself how it was once a gentlemen's sport at Harvard. He cannot know, only dimly fear, that an immigrant socialist will eventually take his place at home. The father who began with the conviction of heroic adventure feels more and more frustrated and insignificant as violent events begin to intrude upon his life. The helplessness of this man who manufactures flags and fireworks is symptomatic of his country drifting in the direction of war. When the father turns to the manufacture of weapons and munitions, he will become himself a victim of the international violence. Near the very end of the novel the narrator provides an extraordinary description of how one passenger from the Lusitania sinks to the ocean floor:

> Poor Father, I see his final exploration. He arrives at the
> new place, his hair risen in astonishment, his mouth and
> eyes dumb. His toe scuffs a soft storm of sand, he kneels
> and his arms spread in pantomimic celebration, the immi-
> grant, as in every moment of his life, arriving eternally on
> the shore of his Self. (269).

Thus the father of the narrator becomes himself an immigrant to the land of death, and the "full self" he had always hoped to reach becomes an image of the final desolation.

The failure of the confident explorer is predetermined by the vanity of his ambitions and the blindness of his conduct. At the beginning of the novel the father of the narrator takes his wealth and power for granted. He supports the proud gestures of Teddy Roosevelt without thinking about the poor immigrants in America who cannot share in the masculine vanity of hunting parties and polar expeditions. The man in the White House is a Republican and all seems right with the world. But not for long. The novel dramatizes life in the tenements of New York and labor conditions in the textile mills of Massachusetts. Everything that the narrator's father would not recognize will soon gather sufficient momentum to overwhelm him. His wife adopts a black child and will later marry a Jewish socialist. Weapons for the revolution are manufactured, without the father knowing about it, right in his own factory. His brother-in-law who sides completely with the rights of the oppressed makes the final judgment—"You have traveled everywhere and learned nothing." His last journey, vain and blind as usual, takes him to his reward on the ocean floor.

All of the quests in the novel, with the exception of the immigrant father's success in Hollywood, prove inconclusive and unsatisfactory. Commander Peary, for example, has spent most of his life planning for the moment of victory when he can be the first man to stand at the very top of the earth. But his triumph is uncertain:

> All day long Peary shuffled back and forth over the ice, a
> mile one way, two miles another, and made his observa-
> tions. No one observation satisfied him. He would walk a
> few steps due north and find himself going due south. On
> this watery planet the sliding sea refused to be fixed. He
> couldn't find the exact place to say this spot, here, is the
> North Pole. (67-68)

The anticlimatic nature of Peary's quest is typical of what happens to the many adventurers in Doctorow's novel. Morgan expects to receive signs from Osiris in the Great Pyramid of Egypt. Instead, he finds himself covered with bedbugs. Coalhouse Walker would like to have his automobile restored in a symbolic gesture of civil and racial justice. Instead, he is shot by the police when he steps from the Morgan Library. Houdini intends to prove his strength by escaping from a buried coffin. Instead, he discovers that the weight of the earth is too much, and he must be dug from the grave by his desperate assistants.

Why do all of the adventures prove inconclusive? It is the narrator of the novel who clearly perceives the mutability of all things. Skating on the pond near his home the young boy watches "only the tracks made by the skaters, traces quickly erased of moments past, journeys taken" (99). The novel is a vision of the many journeys and moments traced on the melting ice. It is his sense of the world in flux that informs the narrator's description of Peary's attempt to locate the North Pole—"On this watery planet the sliding sea refused to be fixed." And just as Peary "shuffled back and forth over the ice" at the inconclusive height of his quest, J. P. Morgan is described as moving blindly about in the King's Chamber of the Great Pyramid—"He paced from the west to the east, from the north to the south, though he didn't know which was which."

While the narrator of the novel recognizes that history is a comic mirror, many of the characters in the book believe in the illusions of themselves cast back by the changing times. J. P. Morgan, for example, believes that Henry Ford and himself are reincarnations of the great pharoahs who commanded the building of the pyramids. Morgan's attempt to convince Ford that he is the reincarnation of a pharoah of the 19th dynasty is one of the finest comic moments in the novel. It turns out that Henry Ford already believes in reincarnation, but not as the result of many years and countless fortunes invested in antiquarian research. Instead, he has invested twenty-five cents in a small book called *An Eastern Fakir's Eternal Wisdom* published by the Franklin Novelty Company of Philadelphia. Ford is perfectly willing to concede his "awesome lineage," but his interest in the mummy of Seti the First is slight, and poor J. P. Morgan will have to journey to Egypt alone.

The narrator of *Ragtime* explains how Morgan is trying to escape from a world of mutability: "His desperate studies settled, inevitably, on the civilizations of ancient Egypt, wherein it was taught that the universe is changeless and that death is followed by the resumption of life" (118). But the novel at every turn reveals the vanity of Morgan's thesis. Nothing is permanent in a world that "refused to be fixed," and all of the adventurers are trapped by the illusions of self cast back by the turning mirror of history. The one successful character in the novel is therefore the immigrant father who can rise to power and fortune in Hollywood because he knows that history is a reel of illusions.

Although it is accepted by Morgan as "an indisputable truth" that he has "no peers," his ancestors are comically revealed in a dream during the cold night in the pyramid. "He dreamed of an ancient life in which he squatted in the bazaars, a peddler exchanging good-natured curses with the dragomans." Morgan would like to believe that he belongs to a "sacred tribe of heroes," but his descent from the great pharoahs is mocked and denied by his dream of the peddler in the bazaar. He attempts to dismiss the dream as a "false sign," but it is the only true image of the financier that the mirror of history will shadow forth.

Even the master of illusion, Harry Houdini, also becomes its victim. All of his staged escapes are mere vaudeville tricks unless Houdini can escape from death itself. After his mother dies Houdini desperately wants to believe in the possibility of some form of supernatural life. But his visits to spiritualists and other conductors of seances all over America only convince him of their fraud and vanity. He wages a national campaign against their trickery with all of the outrage and hurt of a child who has just seen that the wizard is a humbug. Houdini may escape from jails and straightjackets and a Chinese torture machine; he may be among the first to climb into the air at the controls of his own plane; he may hang upside down eleven stories over Times Square; but the only time in his life when a true key to the future is placed in his hands Houdini does not recognize its value until it is too late. He remains just as locked in mortal time as Morgan and Peary. Only the little boy who told him years in advance to "Warn the Duke" will be able to separate from himself in order to put together the novel of illusions.

Houdini's attempt to break from the confinement of a buried coffin is described very early in the novel:

> He was buried alive in a grave and could not escape, and
> had to be rescued. Hurriedly, they dug him out. The earth
> is too heavy, he said gasping. His nails bled. Soil fell from
> his eyes. He was drained of color and couldn't stand. (7)

Some characters in the novel, nevertheless, enjoy being buried alive. The little boy and his stepsister play on the beach by covering one another with sand. "The burial game," the narrator remembers, "was their most serious pleasure." They lie on the beach under sculptured images of their bodies, much like the mummy of the pharoah in his sculptured coffin, until they escape from the mound of sand and run to wash themselves in the ocean. This ritual escape from burial is sought in vain by Houdini and Morgan. Only the children of the novel, especially the narrator as the little boy, can break free from the mold of self and then baptize their new lives.

All of the inconclusive quests in the novel are symptoms of the frustration and supressed violence that will explode at the end of the book with the start of World War I. The decade of tension prior to the war is characterized by the very title of the novel, and also by the life of the great composer, Scott Joplin, who led the way in the creation of ragtime music. His words are used for the epigraph to Doctorow's novel, and his career is echoed throughout *Ragtime*.

Although critics have rightly pointed to Heinrich von Kleist's *Michael Kohlhaas* as a probable source for the character and predicament of Coalhouse Walker, there are also many similarities between Doctorow's jazz pianist and the career of Scott Joplin.[4] In the narrator's home in New Rochelle it is Coalhouse Walker who plays some of the famous Joplin pieces such as "Wall Street Rag" and "The Maple Leaf Rag." After the fire station of New Rochelle is destroyed by the vengeance of Coalhouse Walker, and the newspapers of New York are competing with one another for news of the black terrorist, a picture of Scott Joplin is mistakenly printed by Hearst's *American*. Doctorow allows history and fiction to mirror one another until the reflections become interchangeable. Joplin and Walker are both reported to have come from St. Louis to New York at about the same time. Joplin's opera, *Treemonisha*, tells the story of a dark skinned infant discovered beneath a tree. The child in the opera matures through adversity to become a symbol of black pride and triumph. Coalhouse Walker's son in *Ragtime* is found buried alive near the maple trees in the garden of the narrator's boyhood home. Rescued by the narrator's mother, the black child will be adopted by the narrator's family, and eventually become the minority hero of a series of films created in Hollywood by his third father. The dark child's resurrection from a shallow grave relates him symbolically to the other two children in the novel who play their burial games. The future belongs to all three children, boy and girl, black and white, who will live together in Hollywood, and serve as models for a popular film series. Their lives are thus projected by the mirrors of countless reruns into the unknown future.

Although the children in the opera and the novel live happily ever after, their fathers, with the exception of the immigrant socialist, come to violent ends. The tragic conclusion of Joplin's career is reflected in Doctorow's novel by the misfortune and death of Coalhouse Walker. More than five hundred pieces of music, including a ballet and two operas, were composed by Joplin, but his popularity rested largely upon a few pieces like "The Maple Leaf Rag." He sought in vain for a producer in New York to stage *Treemonisha*. Bitterness and disappointment convinced Joplin that racial prejudice was the cause of his rejection as a serious composer. After years of extraordinary creativity and extreme frustration, Joplin was committed to a mental hospital. While the tension of Doctorow's novel is released in the madness of a world plunged into war, Joplin dies offstage in the mental asylum. But his counterpart in the novel, Coalhouse Walker, directs a violent challenge to the bigotry and conceit of the white community. Walker's threat to blow up the Morgan Library is the occasion for Doctorow to create the novel's most dramatic scene of revolutionary theater. Coalhouse Walker does not survive his violent protest, but the revolution will be continued, and eventually, in 1972, a successful production of *Treemonisha* will be staged in New York. *The Collected Works of Scott Joplin* were published in the same year, and thus E. L. Doctorow was prepared to write *Ragtime*.

The rhythms of violence and rebirth are syncopated in Doctorow's novel like the rich interplay of recurring themes and melodies in ragtime music. The subtlety of its narrative strategy and the complex arrangement of its mirrored images are in harmony with the words of Scott Joplin which Doctorow uses as the epigraph for his novel: "Do not play this piece fast. It is never right to play Ragtime fast."

Notes

[1] "PW Interviews," *Publishers Weekly*, 30 June 1975, pp. 6-7.

[2] E. L. Doctorow, *Ragtime* (New York: Random House, 1975), p. 96. All further references to this edition are cited parenthetically.

[3] Martin Green, *American Scholar*, 45 (Winter 1975-76), p. 841.

[4] See Joan Ditsky, "The German Source of *Ragtime*," *Ontario Review* (Spring-Summer 1976), pp. 84-86, and Walter Knorr, "Doctorow and Kleist: Kohlhass in *Ragtime*," *Modern Fiction Studies*, 22 (1976), pp. 224-227.

1976

John Hawkes
Travesty

John Hawkes is the Edgar Allan Poe of the twentieth century. His novels are as hypnotic and disturbing as the nightmare images of "The City in the Sea" or "The Masque of the Red Death." His narrators and characters are as self-destructive as William Wilson or Roderick Usher. His foreign settings recall the gothic scenes of Poe's fantasy. Necrophilia, schizophrenia, cannibalism—these are the familiar subjects in the illuminated hell of Hawkes and Poe. Their fiction is a replay of "distorted psychic materials" which reveal the "violence and grotesque humor" of nightmares.[1] While the gothic muse of Poe is buried alive in a vault or tomb, Hawkes openly claims that his art is a revenge against the traumas of childhood. A recent critic has declared that Hawkes "has no equal for the communication of revolting, inescapable terror."[2] No equal, except for Edgar Allan Poe.

The fiction of John Hawkes from *The Cannibal* (1949) to *Virginie: Her Two Lives* (1982) is a psychological tour de force, but the novel which best reveals his kinship with the haunted mind of Poe is *Travesty*. The subject of this short novel is the relationship of art and death—or "design and debris" as the suicidal narrator would say while driving his car at high speed into a stone wall. The spirit of Edgar Allan Poe is everywhere in *Travesty* from the narrator in his death machine to the mysterious Tara "where the lady of the dark château lies dreaming."[3] The landscape of nightmare, the monologue of desperate ratiocination, the narrator as psychopath, murderer, and artist—in this novel Hawkes and Poe are fellow travelers into the darkness.

The first epigraph to *Travesty*—"I am imbued with the notion

that a Muse is necessarily a dead woman"—comes from Michel
Leiris's *Manhood*, but it is Poe in *The Philosophy of Composition* who
identifies "the death of a beautiful woman" as "the most poetical topic
in the world." Madeline of Usher, Ligeia, Ulalume, Lenore—the muse
for Poe is always the haunting vision of love and death. The narrator
of *Travesty* advertises himself as "a specialist on the subject of dead
passion" and "an aesthetician of death at high speed." He is especially
pleased to imagine that his suicide and murder will be a tribute to the
woman sleeping in the dark château. Near the end of his journey the
narrator identifies the woman as "the source of my private apocalypse" (125).

Poe may pretend in *The Philosophy of Composition* that his choice
of subject matter is always deliberate and rational, but the repetition
of haunting images in his work implies their compulsive nature. What
he did have to choose, however, was a suitable gothic setting for the
ghosts of the mind to inhabit. Where in 19th century America could
he find a setting for his fiction that would evoke a history of evil and
horror? Hawthorne and James were also concerned with this problem, and often turned to Europe for the solution. Poe had lived in
England as a child, and the mysterious boarding school in "William
Wilson" is drawn from memory, but it is more common for Poe to
borrow the trappings of gothic fiction: a dungeon, a remote sepulcher,
a wild and desolate abbey, the melancholy House of Usher. The name
of the country may vary—Spain, Germany, England—but the focus
seldom moves from "images of the desolate or terrible."

The number of gothic settings available in the next century
would not be any greater. Only a southern writer like Faulkner could
find a usable past of decadent and haunted plantations. Otherwise the
lengthening shadow of American history has not been particularly
hospitable. It is a paradox of our literature that America remains the
country of the future—the territory ahead—despite the vanishing of
the frontier. Hawkes could follow the lead of Poe by turning to
Germany and England for his landscape of terror, but then he still had
to refurbish the gothic imagination for the twentieth century. He
couldn't use the torture chambers of the Inquisition, but a decaying
Nazi asylum in *The Cannibal* does just as well. He couldn't rebuild the
House of Usher, but the survivors of a bombed London serve his
purpose in *The Lime Twig*. War ravaged countries—Germany, Italy,
England—are convenient settings for the distorted psychic materials

liberated from Hawkes's unconscious.

The purest gothic setting is to be found in *Travesty*. The short novel takes place entirely at night. The narrator is driving his car at high speed through a mysterious and deserted countryside. The action presumably takes place in France because a small village is identified as La Roche, but the landscape is more mental than physical, and the narrator even admits that he has never been to the one village that he does name. The chief landmarks in the setting are the dark château where the wife of the narrator is sleeping, the old Roman viaduct which spans a deep gorge, and the stone wall towards which the car is speeding. The château is the familiar home of Ligeia and Madeline. With its "magnificent shutters drawn closed" it is the still living tomb of the gothic muse. The old Roman viaduct is the narrow and precarious bridge across the deep gorge of the unconscious. Although the narrator feels tempted to "sail directly into the wilderness of that deep gorge like some stricken winged demon from the books of childhood," he plans instead to drive the car across the viaduct and then crash at full speed into the stone wall. Any reader of "The Pit and the Pendulum" or "The Cask of Amontillado" will recognize the wall as the chosen symbol of death.

The fiction of Poe and Hawkes typically comes in the form of a short story or a very short novel. *Travesty* is only one hundred and twenty-eight pages. The brevity of their work is dictated by a focus on extreme states of mind and a concentrated poetic style. The first creative experience for Poe and Hawkes was the writing of poetry, and the force of that apprenticeship is clearly visible in their prose. "If any literary work is too long to be read at one sitting," Poe argues in *The Philosophy of Composition*, then it will lose "the immensely important effect derivable from unity of impression."[4] He is talking about the composition of a poem, "The Raven," but the effect of any gothic narrative depends upon its spell not being interrupted. No daylight can be allowed to break into "The Fall of the House of Usher" or into *Travesty*. Hawkes therefore imposes radical limits upon his short novel. Only the narrator is allowed to speak. The sound of his voice is like the hypnotic drone of the racing engine. The first word of the novel is "No," the last word is "None," the injunction observed in between is "Hands off the wheel." Nothing is allowed to disturb the "unity of impression." The monologue can be read at one sitting, and even the classical unities of time, place, and action are observed.

Hawkes is right to describe *Travesty* as: "the purest fiction I've written, and probably the most powerful."[5]

Unity is primarily achieved by limiting the novel to the voice of the desperate narrator. Several of Poe's short stories—"Ligeia," "The Imp of the Perverse," "Berenice"—are constructed in this manner. The solitary narrative voice often comes from a speaker in a very disturbed mental condition. The narrator of "Ligeia" is the victim of "wild visions, opium-engendered." The narrator of "The Imp of the Perverse" is a murderer who speaks to us from the "cell of the condemned." The unnamed speaker of *Travesty* plans to commit both suicide and murder. His friend and daughter are in the speeding car, and the narrator at the wheel promises "there shall be no survivors." Because the perspective is limited to the desperate point of view of the narrator, we have nothing beyond his own words to measure the action of the novel. Some critics have even wondered if the other two passengers in the car really exist, or if they are merely imagined by the driver.[6] Their status is just as ambiguous as the final appearance of the dead wife in "Ligeia." Perhaps the whole novel is the nightmare of the mad narrator. Or perhaps it is the vision of the gothic muse asleep in the dark château who dreams of her husband, daughter, and lover all converging in the night. Hawkes's fiction is open to such interpretation because all "reality" in the psychic monologue is suspect. The "unity of impression" in Poe and Hawkes is ultimately powerful because the fiction invites the reader into the maelstrom of the narrator's psyche. As the ground for each interpretation subtly gives way to the next, the reader is drawn into the infinite regression of the gothic imagination.

A recent critic of *Travesty* argues that: "An author's power can in some sense be measured by the reader's feeling of being 'caught' inside the text."[7] This is particularly true of Hawkes and Poe because the reader cannot escape from the strange voice of the unreliable narrator. We are challenged to discover motivation and meaning where the normal landmarks for such judgment are missing. The monologue in *Travesty* more often than not is set up to frustrate our expectations. Although the narrator is presumably speaking to his friend and daughter in the car, the voice we hear keeps answering the questions that we may be thinking or refuting the conclusions that we may have just reached. As soon as we decide that the narrator at the wheel of the speeding car must be mad, he declares that "I am not merely some sort of suicidal maniac." As soon as we think that his action is motivated by vengeance and jealousy, he dismisses our thought with scorn and pity: "After all I have said . . . you are finally willing to accuse me of mere jealousy?" All of his disclaimers, of course, are suspect, but the monologue never allows us sufficient pause or distance to judge. It is no surprise that Tony Tanner's review of *Travesty* in the *New York Times Book Review* is entitled "John Hawkes: no instructions how to read."

The challenge for the reader of *Travesty* is underscored by Hawkes in a recent interview: "It seems to me necessary to live by creating our own contexts within the constant knowledge of the imminence of annihilation."[8] We appear to be trapped in the car with a mad driver, and must discover for ourselves the method of his madness, if any, before reaching the stone wall. "Ours is the power," insists the narrator, "to invent the very world we are quitting" (57). No fashionable theory about "affective stylistics" is needed to recognize how the reader is taken along for the psychological ride, and must create his own understanding of it at high speed. Gothic fiction has always worked as a psychological attack on the reader, and Donald Greiner is right to maintain that all of Hawkes's novels "involve the reader in the creative process."[9] *Travesty* with its nightmare setting and unreliable narrator is merely the extreme test.

Paul Emmett argues in "The Reader's Voyage Through *Travesty*" that our interest becomes epistemological because we "must get beyond the narrator's methods of knowing."[10] This can only be done by imposing upon the novel a preconceived design. Emmett, for example, uses the archetypal theory of Carl Jung, and thus finds in *Travesty* several correspondences. Enid Veron applies the comic design of Northrop Frye, and thus identifies the narrator as a scapegoat who must be expelled from the community. Plenty of clues may be found in the text to support these interpretations. Not to mention several others. The game is endless because in terms of the text it is not possible to get beyond the narrator's methods of knowing.

The tantalizing quality of gothic fiction often tempts critics to see through the text to the actual psyche of the author. Seldom, however, does such indirect psychoanalysis prove convincing. While some critics are still sifting through the ruins of the House of Usher for the lost patrimony of the author, others are digging in the graves of Ulalume or Annabel Lee for the corpse of Poe's lost mother. The

importance of the ruined house and empty tomb may still echo in the
gothic imagination of Hawkes. The first epigraph to *Travesty* does
announce "that ultimately one can write only to fill a void." The
narrator does claim that "nothing is more important than the existence
of what does not exist" (57). This paradox is at the heart of the theory
of psychological repression, but if it is applied to the fiction of Hawkes,
what will critics find beneath the masquerade of his art? What void
has he attempted to fill? The author, no doubt, may look forward to
the ransacking of his family closet for hints of cannibals, murderers,
and suicidal maniacs. Imagine the special session at some future MLA
to discuss the woman in the dark château! Mockery is not likely to
deter the psychologically intrepid. Hawkes cannot escape the inheritance of Poe.

The characters in *Travesty*, if there are any, are subject to the
same uncertain psychological status. The friend of the narrator, for
example, can easily be viewed as his double. The friend has been
released from a hospital for the insane where the narrator no doubt
belongs. The friend is a bad poet, while the narrator is an artist of
suicide and murder. Both men share the woman who sleeps in the
dark château. The friend also enjoys a sexual relationship with the
narrator's daughter, thus serving as a model for whatever oedipal
wishes the narrator may desire to hide. The men even share the same
astrological sign. If the car hits the stone wall according to plan, the
narrator and his double will die simultaneously. This gothic situation
is familiar to readers of Dostoyevsky or Poe. The double in "William
Wilson" is similar to the friend in *Travesty* in several ways, not the least
of which is that both serve to provoke their respective narrators into
a full disclosure of their murderous intentions.

Such disclosures in gothic fiction are apt to come in a most
peculiar tone of voice. Hawkes's *Travesty* is no exception. The narrator
sounds very calm when we expect him to be the most excited. The car
is traveling at a reckless speed, but the driver talks in a leisurely
fashion as if time were of no concern. The effect is just like a
conversation in a nightmare where time and space are strangely out of
joint. The narrator also sounds very polite when we might expect him
to be hostile and rude. The closer he comes to fulfilling his murderous
intentions, the more solicitous he appears to be of his victim's comfort:
"I am the kindest man you will ever meet." The effect is reminiscent
of Othello choosing the softest way to murder the sleeping Desde-

mona. But the jealous narrator of *Travesty* only sounds tender and thoughtful. Death will still come with the crash against the stone wall.

Perhaps the oddest feature of the narrator's tone is its forced merriment. He often jokes about his victims, calling his chief rival "*cher ami*" or his daughter a "porno brat." The laughter may be heard as a symptom of the hysteria which his calm and polite manner otherwise is trying to cover. Romeo also jokes about himself as a dead man burying the dead, and then he asks: "How oft when men are at the point of death/Have they been merry! Which their keepers call/A lightning before death." Hawkes's novel likewise turns on the paradox of love and death, and it is filled with such lightning. The forced merriment of the narrator is often like the grin of death approaching at the end of the road.

The narrator's voice becomes a positive torment to his captive audience. His friend and daughter are nearly frightened to death, one hardly able to breath in the front seat, the other vomiting in back, while the narrator calmly discusses the artistic design of accidents or his taste for flute music. His philosophical discussion may be intended as a cruel and outrageous monologue, or he may be simply oblivious to the gap between his rhetoric and reality. In either case the effect is that of being held under the spell of a madman. The narrator of Poe's "Imp of the Perverse" speaks in the same fashion when he delivers a scientific lecture on the instinct which has led him to murder and confession. The narrative tone of Hawkes and Poe often echoes with the narcissism of a criminal mind. It is heard in *The Cannibal* when the narrator who plans to be the next leader of Germany discusses his dream of murder and power. The tone is resonant with a mixture of self love and hate. It is heard in *Travesty* when the narrator refers to himself as a "tasteful executioner." And it is adopted by several of Poe's narrators and characters who revel in their damnation.

The narcissist and the criminal in gothic literature often use the power of reason in the service of preserving their chief lies. Thus the narrator of *Travesty* rationalizes at great length in order to masquerade his suicide and murder in terms of a profound artistic and philosophical design. The narrator of Poe's "Descent into the Maelstrom" likewise holds a discourse on the principles of Archimedes while being sucked deeper into the whirlpool. It is characteristic of Poe's imagination to harness the powers of rationalization to impose a kind of false logic upon an irrational world. Consider the calm deliberations of his master detective, C. August Dupin, in the midst of crime and violence. Hawkes also has the peculiar talent to convince us that chaos has an irresistible order. *The Cannibal, Blood Oranges, Travesty*—his nightmare vision reaches to the calm at the center of madness.

The calm is always deceptive. It is the false composure of the driver who takes us past the dark château, over the narrow viaduct, towards the stone wall. Of course we should not confuse the author with his desperate narrator, but there is not much relief in thinking of Hawkes at the wheel of his fiction when he admits that "everything I've written comes out of nightmare."[11] How can we possibly agree with Albert Guerard that "*Travesty* is a masterpiece of wholly conscious and controlled, truly classical art?"[12] It was Poe who liked to pretend that his gothic fiction was created in a fully rational manner. *The Philosophy of Composition* is a remarkable effort to prove that the composition of "The Raven" was wholly conscious and controlled. Whether Poe was trying to fool his audience, or was merely fooling himself, we cannot know, but *The Philosophy of Composition* stands as a critical reminder that any effort to pass off gothic art as "classical" is apt to be a travesty.

Although the fiction of John Hawkes is rooted in the abnormal and irrational, it is nevertheless composed of clear and precise images. Hawkes shares with Poe the ability to conjure images of terror that are especially powerful because of their detail and particularity. The scene of the Duke dissecting the little boy in *The Cannibal* is remarkable for its precision and its fastitious tone. The narrator of *Travesty* seems almost clairvoyant as he imagines the "design and debris" of the impending crash. The most effective horror for the gothic imagination is to have the specter of some implacable fate dawn upon the consciousness in slow motion. This is what happens in "The Fall of the House of Usher" when Roderick first hears the sounds of Madeline in her subterranean coffin. And this is what happens in *Travesty* when the narrator gradually convinces his terrified passengers that the stone wall is approaching.

The narrator thinks of himself as a privileged man, an artist imposing form upon chaos. His hands are on the wheel, his voice is heard exclusively, but he cannot escape the driving force of his own psychic needs. The monologue is dominated by visions of sex and death. Marcus Klein has argued convincingly that the narrator, "far from being a supreme imposer of forms, is a desperate compromiser."[13] The narrator is thus a parody of the gothic artist who wants to believe that nightmares are designs of human will. Roderick Usher is also the victim of his own art. He writes poems and draws pictures that illustrate over and over again the specter that will not stay buried in his soul. The narrator of *Travesty* is a comic descendent of Roderick. He also is hypersensitive to sound, but instead of hearing his sister open her coffin in the cellar, he hears the muffled vomiting of his daughter in the back seat. The abnormal sensitivity of the narrator is further revealed in comic fashion when he confesses: "I suffer acutely because one of my ears is always colder than the other" (44). Just what his terrified passengers have always wanted to hear!

The friend who visits Roderick in hopes of distracting him from his desperate state of mind is drawn instead into the melancholy and "insufferable gloom" of the House of Usher. He too is forced to see the "enshrouded figure of the lady Madeline." His own healthy composure is destroyed, and he barely escapes with his life as he flees from the gothic ruin. The victims in the speeding car of Hawkes's narrator are not so lucky. Only the reader is held captive to the haunted mind of a gothic artist, and then released just in time to listen for the crash. The car in *Travesty* is analogous to the house in Poe's tale—the psychological image of its inhabitant. At the end of "The Fall of the House of Usher" the narrator looks back just in time to see the "mighty walls rushing asunder." On the title page of Hawkes's novel the reader encounters a photograph of the shattered automobile.

"The true purpose of the novel," wrote John Hawkes in 1962, is "to objectify the terrifying similarity between the unconscious desires of the solitary man and the disruptive needs of the visible world."[14] From the hunger of the Duke in *The Cannibal* to the cruelty of Seigneur in *Virginie: Her Two Lives*, the desires of the solitary man have been graphically dramatized, but what does Hawkes mean by "the disruptive needs of the visible world?" Does he want to imply that cannibalism and torture are somehow the requirements of nature? If the visible world has such needs then the individual is neither solitary nor responsible. Thus the narrator of *Travesty* declares that: "No man is guilty of anything, whatever he does." This statement is characteristic of the author who declares: "I want my fiction to destroy conventional morality and conventional attitudes," but it begs the question of how far the gothic attack can be carried against the reader.[15]

If it can be accepted that the psychic needs of the characters in

Hawkes's fiction are somehow universal in human nature, then no limit exists to their fascination and power. This is precisely the argument adopted by several of Hawkes's most eloquent supporters. The unconscious roots of his fictional characters have been repeatedly studied—"Hawkes's people are the monsters of the mind"—and the common inheritance of his terror has been acknowledged—"Hawkes is the poet of our dread."[16] This view assumes that the shapes of fear and terror in the gothic imagination are the common property of all readers. "The world of a Hawkes novel," wrote Charles Matthews in 1963, "is our own inner world, and the nightmare landscapes are familiar to us from our own nightmares."[17] Albert Guerard makes the same point in his influential essay, "The Prose Style of John Hawkes." He describes the work of Hawkes correctly as "a fictional world in which violence, anxiety, and regression are everyday norms," and then he boldly assumes "this is our underground life."[18]

Hawkes himself has attempted to promote the same assumption in several interviews. "I'm convinced," he said in 1965 "that considerable numbers of people in this country must have imaginative needs quite similar to mine."[19] "The writer who exploits his own psychic life," he said in 1971, "reveals the inner lives of us all, the inner chaos, the negative aspects of the personality in general."[20]

This assumption has not gone unchallenged. Just as Poe was attacked by some of his contemporaries as a cruel imposter, Hawkes has been accused of a "contemptible imagination" and dismissed as "more an unadmitted voyeur of horror than its calm delineator."[21] Worse than being criticized, as Poe unfortunately knew, is to be excluded. The critical acceptance of Hawkes also is marked by some notable lapses. Jonathan Baumbach, for example, chose not to include Hawkes in his 1965 study of contemporary American fiction. Despite the title of the study, *The Landscape of Nightmare*, and its claim to explore the "underside of consciousness," the novels of Hawkes were dismissed as "so many eccentric exercises."[22] What happens then to Hawkes's claim to be representing "personality in general"?

The debate between the champions and detractors of Hawkes amounts to more than a difference in literary taste. At the heart of the controversy is a disagreement about psychological theory. On the one hand are critics who accept Jung's theory of the collective unconscious, and thus are prepared to argue that the nightmare images of Hawkes's fiction are the common property of human nature. This theory, of course, has been especially useful for many apologists of symbolic literature. On the other hand are critics who question Jung's theory, and feel instead that the images of gothic fiction, however clear and brilliant, represent a disturbed and narrow range of the psyche. If the idea of the collective unconscious is discounted, gothic literature may still be enjoyed for its unusual images of fear and terror, but it cannot be accepted as an expression of "the inner lives of us all."

The most explicit Jungian interpretation of *Travesty* is by Paul Emmett. He typically describes the novel as "the mythic voyage of the narrator" which reveals "the universal elements of the unconscious."[23] Whose unconscious? What universal elements? Why should the desperate and maniacal narrator of *Travesty* be treated as Everyman? "The child awakes in us once again," says the narrator, "when we drive at night" (28). Even if this premise is accepted, does it follow that all children have the same psychic experience? How can we possibly know if Emmett is right when he claims that the goal of the narrator in *Travesty* is to rediscover the lost innocence of the "pre-natal collective unconscious?" Jung and Freud may assume that children have the same pre-natal psychic experience, but what happens when this theory is applied to the work of a writer like Hawkes who openly claims that "fiction should achieve revenge for all the indignities of our childhood?" Few readers of *The Passion Artist* are likely to identify with the outrages suffered by the child in that remarkable novel. Any theory which reduces all psychic experience to some uniform model fails to do justice to the rich, bizarre, and striking originality of Hawkes's work.

There is always the possibility, of course, that the critics who charge Poe or Hawkes with a "contemptible imagination" are protesting too much, and ironically proving the common psychological inheritance which they would rather deny. Any attempt to disown the specters of the gothic imagination can always be explained as a form of psychological repression. Indeed, the public rejection of Poe and Hawkes could be interpreted as a defense mechanism against the hidden fears in the "collective unconscious." If the gothic artist is able to create "fierce verbal equivalents of deep-locked psychic history," then it would be natural for the public to be wary of such writers.[24] Poe was often mistreated by his contemporaries, and Hawkes once was called "the least read novelist of substantial merit in the United States."[25] To explain their fate, however, with the psychological theory of repression is too much like special pleading. Doesn't it make more critical and psychological sense to assume that the gothic imagination, however brilliant, may indeed be limited by its eccentricity? That is not to deny Poe and Hawkes a place in American literature, it is merely an attempt to define that place.

After complaining that *Time* and *Newsweek* might never review *Travesty*, Hawkes turned for comfort to the metaphor of psychological repression: "There is probably a strange conspiracy, conscious or not, to keep my work from getting real public attention."[26] Nonsense. The truth of the matter is that John Hawkes has nine novels in print, not to mention several short stories and plays, and his work from the very beginning has found a limited but loyal audience. If large-scale commercial success continues to elude him, it has nothing to do with a conspiracy, conscious or not, it is simply the result of the different and original focus of his writing. *Travesty* is a remarkable book which deserves to be ranked along with the best gothic fiction of Edgar Allan Poe, but not all readers will care to be a captive audience while the narrator drives at high speed towards a stone wall.

Notes

[1] John Kuehl, *John Hawkes and the Craft of Conflict* (New Brunswick, New Jersey: Rutgers University Press, 1975), p. 9.

[2] David Littlejohn, "The Anti-Realists," *Daedalus*, 92 (Spring 1963), p. 256.

[3] John Hawkes, *Travesty* (New York: New Directions, 1976), p. 121. All further references to this edition are cited parenthetically.

[4] Edgar Allan Poe, *Selected Prose and Poetry* (New York: Holt, Rinehart, and Winston, 1962), p. 421.

[5] *A John Hawkes Symposium: Design and Debris* (New York: New Directions, 1977), p. 174.

[6] See Donald J. Greiner's "Private Apocalypse: The Visions of *Travesty*," *A John Hawkes Symposium*, pp. 142-153.

[7] Charles Baxter, "In the Suicide Seat: Reading John Hawkes's *Travesty*," *Georgia Review* (Winter 1980), p. 871.

[8] Quoted by Paul Emmett, "The Reader's Voyage Through *Travesty*," *Chicago Review* (Fall 1976), p. 177.

[9] Donald J. Greiner, *Comic Terror: The Novels of John Hawkes* (Memphis: Memphis State University Press, 1973), p. 244.

[10] Paul Emmett, *Chicago Review* (Fall 1976), p. 179.

[11] John Hawkes, "The Landscape of the Imagination," unpublished transcript of a BBC recording, November 2, 1966. Quoted by John Kuehl, *John Hawkes and the Craft of Conflict*, p. 3.

[12] *A John Hawkes Symposium*, p. 8.

[13] Marcus Klein, "The Satyr at the Head of the Mob," *A John Hawkes Symposium*, p. 163.

[14] John Hawkes, "Notes on the Wild Goose Chase," *The Massachusetts Review* (Summer 1962), p. 784.

[15] Interview with John Kuehl, November 8, 1971. Quoted by Kuehl, *John Hawkes and the Craft of Conflict*, p. 157.

[16] Frederick Busch, *Hawkes: A Guide to His Fictions* (Syracuse: Syracuse University Press, 1973), pp. xi-xx.

[17] Charles Matthews, "The Destructive Vision of John Hawkes," *Critique* (Fall 1963), p. 38.

[18] Albert J. Guerard, "The Prose Style of John Hawkes," *Critique* (Fall 1963), p. 19.

[19] John Hawkes, "An Interview," *Wisconsin Studies in Contemporary Literature* (Summer 1965), pp. 141-155.

[20] Interview with John Kuehl, November 8, 1971. Quoted by Kuehl, *John Hawkes and the Craft of Conflict*, pp. 164-165.

[21] Roger Sale, "*The Blood Oranges*," *New York Review of Books* (October 1971), pp. 2-6.

[22] Jonathan Baumbach, *Landscape of Nightmare: Studies in the Contemporary American Novel* (New York: University Press, 1965), p. 5.

[23] Paul Emmett, "The Reader's Voyage Through *Travesty*," *Chicago Review* (Fall 1976), p. 180.

[24] Frederick Busch, *Hawkes: A Guide to His Fictions*, p. 172.

[25] Leslie Fiedler, "The Pleasures of John Hawkes," *The Lime Twig* (New York: New Directions, 1961), p. viii.

[26] *A John Hawkes Symposium: Design and Debris*, p. 171.

1977

Philip Roth
The Professor of Desire

"Reality," suggests John Barth, "is a nice place to visit but you wouldn't want to live there."[1] The victim-hero in realistic literature, however, has no choice. He is often trapped in a world he can neither understand nor control. "I think that realistic literature from the first has been a victim literature," declares Saul Bellow, who chose "The Victim" as the title for his second novel.[2] Philip Roth believes that Bellow is "the country's most accomplished working novelist," and he has followed the example of Bellow by creating a series of novels with heroes or heroines who are often victims of themselves: Lucy Nelson in *When She Was Good* (1967) is killed by her own self-righteousness; Trick E. Dixon in *Our Gang* (1971) is suffocated by his own hot air; the victim-hero of *Portnoy's Complaint* (1969) uses his own flesh in a comic orgy of pleasure and guilt; and the most extraordinary victim in modern literature is the hero of *The Breast* (1972) who is transformed in the spirit of Gogol or Kafka into a giant mammary gland. This novella is a monologue of bewildered desire and embarrassment because the victim must live in a reality that he has only dreamed of visiting.

The novels of Philip Roth illustrate a progress in the self-revelation of the victim-hero. No other novelist in the 1970s has experimented more successfully with different ways of projecting the voices of characters who are trapped in a world determined by their own fears and desires. Roth's experiments in narrative structure move away from the conventional form of the realistic novel and explore various ways of presenting dramatic monologues.

When She Was Good is the most conventional novel in this series.

Although much of the story is told from Lucy Nelson's point of view, she is not the narrator, and her self-righteous fury is largely expressed in dialogue. Her fear of a wasted life and her righteous desire to improve or destroy her husband are dramatized in conversations among realistic characters.

Our Gang is more experimental in form. It does not have a narrator, either first or third person, and it does not have any dialogue in the usual form of conversation. Instead, Roth's political satire is a montage of presidential speeches, television announcements, and press conference rhetoric. The only direct statements from the author are the few italicized stage directions. The reader thus receives a dramatic illusion of political news unfolding as a media event. Roth entertains his audience with comic imitations of public speeches, and is thereby able to satirize what passes for reality in the political life of his nation. Roth's special target for satire is the paranoid and hypo-critical rhetoric of Trick E. Dixon. By casting the novel as a media event Roth has designed a way for the victim-hero to expose himself. The president's fear of political loss and his vengeful desire to silence all opposition are revealed in his own familiar voice.

Portnoy's Complaint is another dramatization of a victim-hero. The title character, however, is not a public figure whose hypocrisy and lust for power can become a media event. How can Roth broadcast the hidden desires and obsessions of a private figure? His solution is to cast the novel in the form of a monologue which Portnoy delivers to his psychoanalyst. The result is a self-revelation of guilt and lust which is dramatized for the reader within the illusion of a realistic patient-doctor relationship. The voice of Portnoy has all the manic fury of a victim who is trapped among the roots of his own psyche. While the patient attempts to impress his analyst with a wild display of shame and pride, the reader is in the position of overhearing a psychological confession. The power of the novel thus comes from the dramatic revelation of fear and desire projected by the voice of the victim-hero.

The Breast follows a similar narrative strategy. The novella is a monologue delivered by the man who has suffered the incredible transformation. He no longer has eyes to see his audience, but he assumes that television cameras are trained upon him and that the whole world must be watching. His voice is therefore addressed beyond the immediate company of his doctor to include "skeptics, friends, students, relatives, colleagues, and all you strangers . . . my fellow mammalians." The victim-hero of *The Breast* is a professor of literature who knows the transformations in the fiction of Gogol and Kafka which foreshadow his own. What he cannot understand is how the impossible events of fiction can now be his reality. And why, of all people, has he, David Kepesh, been singled out to be the subject of this absurd transformation? The comedy of the novella owes much to the disbelief and outrage projected by the voice subject to the "endocrino-pathic catastrophe." The bewildered Kepesh cries, "this isn't happen-ing—it can't . . . it is a physiological and biological and anatomical impossibility." His doctor, however, calmly replies, "How then do you explain your predicament?"

Roth thought for a while about writing a sequel to *The Breast*. Why not dramatize the career of the human dirigible as a side show attraction in the circus of American life? Imagine the giant erogenous zone being interviewed by Johnny Carson and exhibited to thousands at Yankee Stadium. Public desire for the grotesque and the pathetic might support David Kepesh indefinitely as a travelling breast. After a first draft of eighty pages, however, Roth decided to abandon the sequel. In the last few pages of *The Breast* the hero has imagined his possible career as a celebrated public oddity, and Roth came to realize that any extension of this material would be repetitive and pointless. Instead, he began to think about the character and life of David Kepesh before his bizarre transformation. A few realistic details about his life as a professor of literature, a mistress, a father, and a broken marriage had been included in *The Breast*. "The details that had formed the realistic underpinnings of a very surreal story," Roth has explained in an interview, were now "begging to be brought to life, only this time on their own terms."[3] The result is Philip Roth's tenth, and perhaps his best novel, *The Professor of Desire*. Although it appears in 1977, five years after *The Breast*, it tells the story of a younger David Kepesh. Readers who come to *The Professor of Desire* familiar with Roth's earlier work know what a strange fate awaits the victim-hero, but only the last page of this novel hints at the bizarre future. Roth leaves his narrator, fearful of "transformations yet to come," sucking with des-perate frenzy on the breast of his mistress. It is quite possible to read *The Professor of Desire* without knowing about the future. Although the second novel oddly comes as the antecedent of the first, Roth has explained that *The Professor of Desire* "doesn't bear a necessary relationship to *The Breast*," and the two books may be read independently.

The second book is undoubtedly the more successful. Indeed, it may have been written to even the score with the many critics who had dismissed *The Breast* as a mere indulgence of sophomoric humor. Reviews of the earlier book had been entitled "Uplift," "Falsie," "Literary Titillations," and "Braless in Gaza." The reviewers complained that Roth's book was a cheap and vulgar commercial trick. But five years later a novel with the same characters was greeted with superlative reviews. *The Professor of Desire* was hailed by *The New York Times* as one of the most important books of the year. Other critics went further to praise the novel as "one of the most distinguished books of the decade" and "among the major achievements of the literature of our time."[4]

What did Philip Roth achieve with his tenth novel in order to deserve such generous tributes? "The victim," suggests Ihab Hassan, "is the representative hero of our time . . . his condition is simply the test case of our moral and aesthetic life."[5] After writing a series of novels about victim-heroes with narrative voices that sound like cries of the damned—Lucy Nelson, Trick E. Dixon (who literally goes to hell in *Our Gang*), Alexander Portnoy, and David Kepesh—Roth was prepared to create a protagonist who is more complex and sympathetic than any of his predecessors. David Kepesh in *The Professor of Desire* is typically caught between desire and respectability, but his romantic yearnings have the wonderful sadness celebrated by Chekhov, and his feelings of guilt have the oedipal terror invoked by Kafka. The influence of these writers can be projected in *The Professor of Desire* because Roth chooses a narrator who teaches literature, especially the stories and novels of Chekhov and Kafka. It is possible for David Kepesh to compare his own emotions to their fictional prototypes, and thus live in imaginative worlds never visited by Lucy Nelson, Trick E. Dixon, or Alexander Portnoy. The victim-hero of *The Professor of Desire* may still be trapped by his own desires and fears, but his complex understanding of his own plight brings him close to fulfilling the prophecy of Hassan—"his condition is simply the test case of our moral and aesthetic life."

Creating a narrator who teaches literature offers Roth several advantages. The novel can be a monologue of the narrator's thoughts as he brings them together in preparation for one of his classes on the literature of romantic desire. Instead of having a politician explaining himself at a press conference, or a patient confessing his obsessions to his psychoanalyst, Roth can now have a professor exploring his subject with a group of students. If his own life happens to be inextricably mixed up with his subject, so much the better for the dramatic quality of his monologue. At least the voice of the professor is neither limited to the clichés of a politician trying to defend his crookedness, nor to the rationalization of a patient trying to impress his analyst. If the progress of Roth's art can be measured by the extent of consciousness he is able to project in his narrative monologues, then the complex voice of David Kepesh in *The Professor of Desire* indicates the maturity of Roth as a novelist.

Roth prepares us for the full scope of his narrator's reflections by showing us the education of David Kepesh from the time he is a boy of nine years until he is a professor of literature in his mid-thirties. If the form of the novel is a monologue intended as a lecture for the narrator's students, it is only appropriate that the subject of the novel be the education of the professor. The book, however, is more than a typical *Bildungsroman*. Although it shows the growing awareness of the boy as he passes through some of the expected scenes of initiation, it does not end with the usual promise of a bright future. Roth's young hero is also a victim, and his story will end in a twilight mood of helplessness. The familiar narratives of education by Wordsworth and Joyce are only similar to the story of Roth's narrator up to a certain point. The growth of a young poet's mind in *The Prelude*, "fostered alike by beauty and by fear," has much in common with the desire and fear experienced by the growing boy in Roth's novel. The hero of the poem, however, reaches the top of Snowdon and finds the emblem of "majestic intellect," while the victim-hero of the novel vacations in the mountains only to find intimations of his own mortality. Roth's novel differs in the same way from Joyce's *A Portrait of the Artist as a Young Man*. Stephen Dedalus and David Kepesh both experience the growing stages of temptation, but Joyce's hero is ready to go forth at the end of the novel to a new creative life, while Roth's narrator is fearing death and "transformations yet to come."

Roth begins the novel with the word "temptation," and then proceeds to show how the desires of his hero are often in conflict with the fears which echo parental commands. The education of the future professor of literature involves his meeting at each stage of his conflict with a person who not only represents that level of temptation but who also teaches him a form of self-expression that will carry him on to the next stage. Thus the hero of the novel progresses through degrees of erotic experience, and at the same time is learning how to understand and express in words the full scope of his passion. It is not surprising that David Kepesh has a remarkable future as a giant erogenous zone capable of talking!

Roth introduces his narrator as a young boy living with his mother and father at their mountainside resort hotel. The setting is idyllic; the parents are models of propriety—a mother who types neat labels on everything, and a father described as "my Mosaic dad." The first serpent to enter this Eden of David's youth is Herbie Bratasky— "social director, bandleader, crooner, comic, and master of ceremonies" for the summer resort hotel. Herbie has a talent for obscene imitations, and the young narrator is very impressed with such daring attacks upon the respectability of his parent's world. Herbie becomes the boy's hero by tempting him to enjoy the shameful expression of forbidden desires. When a letter comes from Herbie in the winter with more news of vulgar triumphs, the narrator feels both excitement and mortification. His imagination is filled with terror at the thought of the letter being discovered—"mother and father will be shamed forever." The narrator's childhood in Eden cannot survive the lessons of the tempter. Along with the taste of forbidden impulse, he also learns a new mode of self-consciousness. David Kepesh discovers the power that comes from successful imitation. His loss of innocence means the ability to assume a variety of roles. The devil has symbolically entered his life as a "master of ceremonies" and "social director."

Nine years later as a freshman at college the narrator tells us "my penchant for mimicry very nearly equals my mentor's, only instead of imitations à la Bratasky, I do Bratasky, the guests, and the characters on the staff."[6] The narrator has turned his childhood into a self-conscious dramatic charade. It is not surprising that at college he is studying and peforming in the theater. Leading roles in a number of university productions nourish his desire for the spotlight, but a visit from his parents reminds him of the vanity of such "egomaniacal cravings." Although he then turns to the study of European literature, the narrator is still exploring the power of assuming different roles. In vain does he say: "At twenty I must stop impersonating others and Become Myself, or at least begin to impersonate the self I believe I ought now to be" (12). Roth mocks the goal of self-discovery because he knows that David Kepesh can no more resist the multiple selves that come to him from drama and literature than he will be able to control the explosion of hormones that later turn him into a breast. It is the fate of the narrator in all ways to become the reflection of his own desires.

David Kepesh as an undergraduate earns a reputation by imitating Don Juan, but the reputation is based more on words than deeds. His campaign slogan is borrowed from Byron—"Studious by day, dissolute by night." Few girls, however, are convinced by this advertisement. In another English class the narrator comes across a line from Macaulay—"A rake among scholars, a scholar among rakes." Whatever doubtful value these slogans may have in David's campaign for sexual experience, both of the quotations clearly illustrate the conflict in his mind between inhibition and desire. The conflict itself is not remarkable, but it is significant that the narrator is finding words to express his psychological drama. He is on his way toward becoming a talking breast.

The next stage of his education as a professor of desire takes place during a fellowship year in Europe. The narrator meets two Swedish girls, Elizabeth and Birgitta, and almost immediately moves in with them. Soon the three are exploring forms of erotic satisfaction including bondage and masochism. David is so flattered and excited to suddenly have a harem, that he fails to notice how their sexual adventures are pushing one of the girls to the edge of breakdown and suicide. Remorse and temporary impotence are his response to Elizabeth's attempted suicide, but soon his passion to be a master of whores finds satisfaction with Birgitta, and they travel through Europe picking up other casual partners. Although this wild spring of the narrator's desire has been made possible by his distance from parents and school, the fears of his childhood are strong enough to bring him back home to a career as a student and teacher. What he has learned from Elizabeth and Birgitta about the pleasures and pains of erotic adventure will now be shaped by his imagination into part of a monologue eventually intended for his class on romantic literature. Wordsworth claims in *The Prelude* to chart the growth of a poet's mind, but how much does he reveal about his early sexual adventures with Annette Vallon? Roth, however, can exploit the greater candor of recent fiction to provide his narrator with a full apprenticeship in sexual curiosity.

Just as David Kepesh is about to finish his graduate study in comparative literature he meets a more exotic temptress—a beautiful American woman who has lived in Hong Kong for eight years with a man of great wealth and power. Although he tries to understand Helen (Could a temptress be known by any other name?) by comparing her life to places and characters in Conrad and Tolstoy, the narrator cannot help but wonder if Helen's tales of Asiatic splendor have not been plagiarized from *Screen Romance*. Nevertheless, he marries her, and then suffers the fate of being unable to live up to her fantasies. Worse yet, her wild behavior is a violent challenge to his sense of order and discipline. All that he has learned from his parents about responsibility is betrayed by her self-indulgent tantrums. Soon their marriage is a battleground of bitter charges: she mocks him as one of "those poor innocent theoretical bookworms," and he taunts her for acting like "the runner-up for Queen of Tibet." Although she resents being seen as a character in a book, and he resents being scorned as a reader of books, their lives are both hopelessly determined by the attraction of romantic fiction. David's attempt to believe in himself as the husband of the exotic Helen and still complete his graduate study of comparative literature proves to be the most unhappy stage of his development. At least when he crossed the Atlantic to enjoy the first fruits of forbidden pleasure with Elizabeth and Birgitta he could feel the thrill of sensual curiosity, but when he later crosses the Pacific to bring back the runaway Helen, all he can feel is baffled desire and fear for his hopeless marriage.

What distinguishes *The Professor of Desire* from other novels about frustrated love and broken marriages is the way Roth's narrator can learn from his own experience in order to write about "romantic disillusionment" in the work of Chekhov. By creating a narrator who becomes a professor of literature as well as desire, Roth can pretend that life and literature are interchangeable in the pages of his novel. The result is a work of art that contains within itself mirrors of other works of art. Roth's narrator quotes from Chekhov and dreams about Kafka in ways that illuminate his own deepest fears and wishes.

Teaching the stories of Chekhov tempts David Kepesh to daydream in his classroom about his own romantic yearning and troubled sadness. "During the weeks near the end of the term when we study Chekhov's stories, I find, while reading aloud to my students . . . that each and every sentence seems to me to allude to my own plight above all, as though by now every single syllable I think or utter must first trickle down through my troubles" (72). What seems to appeal to David Kepesh most of all is Chekhov's "feel for the disillusioning moment." When he reads aloud from stories such as "About Love" or "Lady with a Lapdog" he responds with sympathy for the sorrow and pathos of romantic disillusionment. After his divorce from Helen the narrator of Roth's novel is left with unhappy and painful memories which he begins to shape into monologues for delivery to his psychiatrist. Roth has considerable practice when it comes to having a fictional narrator dramatize his psychological problems for a bewildered analyst, but Kepesh differs from Portnoy because he himself holds a degree as a doctor of philosophy, and can draw upon the examples of literature to explain his own troubles. At the nadir of his depression, however, he wonders aloud to his psychiatrist if a close identification with books isn't one cause of his plight. "'Perhaps,' I wearily suggest, 'reading books is the opiate of the educated classes.'" Instead of finding comfort in his affinity with the victim-heroes of Chekhov's stories, Roth's narrator feels his own sadness intensified. He cannot tell if life imitates art or vice versa. Perhaps by turning away from books, he thinks in his despair, it may be possible to cancel the sadness of art and life.

The thesis about romantic disillusionment in Chekhov which Kepesh has been trying to reshape into a book is temporarily abandoned during his worst period of depression. Instead, he talks three times a week to his analyst, and finds some distraction with a disreputable colleague who is a reincarnation of Herbie Bratasky. Roth's narrator is amused by the lecherous adventures of his colleague, but he remains too inhibited himself to ever become fully committed to the "libidinous fallacy." At this time he meets a woman who is ready to create with him the kind of comfortable and domestic love that he has not experienced since the death of his mother. It is not long after David has begun to enjoy this happy relationship with Claire that he is able to resume work on his Chekhov manuscript. His original thesis on romantic disillusionment becomes a forty thousand word essay on "license and restraint in Chekhov's world." The book is appropriately dedicated to Claire because it is with her that David finds, temporarily at least, a truce between the desire and fear, the license and restraint, at the root of his psyche.

Near the end of the novel David and Claire spend a summer

together in the countryside of his childhood. Can the innocence of
paradise be regained? David is very moved by the familiar view—"the
gentle green hills and distant green mountains beyond the dormer
windows take me back to the bedroom vista of my childhood." He
feels extraordinary contentment with Claire—"the sense I already
have with her that I am living at last in accordance with my true spirit,
that, indeed, I am 'home'" (196). The summer of happiness is dramatized by scenes of quiet enjoyment, tender companionship, and sensi-
tive fulfillment. There are few scenes elsewhere in Roth's novels, nor
indeed in other fiction of the 1970s, that convey so much warmth and
contentment. But is it possible to find a quiet harbor after the violent
journey of passion with Elizabeth, Birgitta, and Helen? Is it possible
for the voices of temptation, the many voices of Bratasky, to ever be
fully silenced?

Despite his return to the idyllic setting of childhood, David
cannot escape a self-conscious awareness of his own fallen state. Even
his ex-wife makes an unexpected visit to the summer paradise, as if to
remind him of past battles and wounds that will not heal. His father
also comes with an old friend who is a concentration camp survivor.
Roth's narrator has visited the Jewish cemetery in Prague, and placed
a pebble on the grave of Franz Kafka. At that time he realized—"there
are not pebbles enough to go around"—for the Jewish citizens of
Prague exterminated in Trezin, Auschwitz, Belsen and Dachau. Now,
listening to his father's friend tell about the concentration camp, the
fear in David's soul comes to the surface. He is more aware than ever
of mortality, and anxiously wonders if his father will even survive this
visit. His happiness with Claire is disturbed by this elegiac mood, and
the final words of Chekhov's "Lady with a Lapdog" are all he can think
of to indicate the future—"And both of them knew that the most
complicated and difficult part was only just beginning" (260). At this
point in his sad reflections David Kepesh feels that his own life is
helplessly mingled with the shadows and mirrors of Chekhov's fiction. The apples are falling in his orchard, and the season of love will
soon be over. In the twilight of their desire and fear David says to
Claire: "It's a simple Chekhov story, isn't it?"

The rich echoes of Chekhov, however, are only a part of the
consciousness of Roth's narrator. Much of his knowledge about
victims in literature can be traced directly to the life and art of Franz
Kafka. Roth's narrator teaches Kafka to his comparative literature

class, makes a visit to Prague, writes a lecture for an international conference on Kafka, and even dreams about an extraordinary meeting with Kafka's whore. Although he plans to give a lecture on Kafka's "preoccupations with spiritual starvation," what interests David Kepesh the most is the conflict of passion and respectability. He identifies with Kafka's sense "of having been summoned—or of imagining yourself summoned—to a calling that turns out to be beyond you, yet in the face of every compromising or farcical consequence, being unable to wise up and relinquish the goal" (172). If he feels that he has been summoned to a life of erotic adventure—Elizabeth, Birgitta, and Helen—he knows that he can neither satisfy their romantic fantasies, nor be content with the quiet, domestic love offered by Claire. Thus he identifies with the many victim-heroes of Kafka's fiction who seem to be "banging their heads against invisible walls."

The invisible wall, more often than not, is the voice of parental admonition. Abe Kepesh may be less threatening than the images of authority that haunt Kafka's fiction, but the father of Roth's narrator is still a strong influence on the psyche of the victim-hero. "Abe" does not sound as authoritative as "Abraham," but Roth does imply that once again the child may be prepared for sacrifice to the father's sense of obedience. "The question of who or what shall have influence and jurisdiction over one's life," writes Philip Roth, "has been a concern in much of my work. From whom shall one receive the Commandments?"[7] The commands in *The Professor of Desire* are received from the narrator's father in the mountainside castle of his youth. Fear and guilt are then part of the psyche of the victim-hero no matter where he travels in search of passion. Readmittance to the castle is never possible. Instead of inheriting his father's property, it is sold to strangers and sadly transformed. Kafka admits in the "Letter to his Father" that "marrying is barred to me because it is your very own domain." Roth's narrator at the end of the novel likewise feels that marriage to Claire is impossible. The oedipal conflict of fear and desire is central in the fiction of Kafka and Roth. "My writing was all about you," Kafka confesses to his father, "it was an intentionally long-drawn-out leave-taking from you."[8] In the final scene of Roth's novel the narrator is listening anxiously for the death rattle of Abraham.

Roth uses Kafka in two further ways to mirror the desire and fear of his victim-hero. Although the novel is largely realistic in tone and action, *The Professor of Desire* does contain two important scenes which draw upon the surrealist tendencies of Kafka's art. The first is an extraordinary dream sequence that takes place during the narrator's visit to Prague. After touring the city and the cemetery, he has a wild dream about visiting an old woman who claims to have been the prostitute who satisfied the desires of Kafka. In the dream the tour guide to this venereal wonder is Herbie Bratasky, the first tempter in the Eden of David's childhood. The whore, of course, is named Eva. Herbie is still the master of ceremonies, but he refuses to translate the words of Eva just as she is about to reveal what she did for Kafka to give him the most pleasure. "*What was it?*" cries David with extreme frustration. Typically, however, he is not allowed to have any knowledge of the primal scene. "Oh," says Herbie, "I don't think your dad would want you to hear that, Dave. Or your dad's dad, and so on, all the way back to the Father of the Faithful and the Friend of God" (193). In his dreams David is thus the pathetic victim of frustrated desire and the admonitions of all the patriarchs.

The final Kafka twist to Roth's novel is the narrator's "fear of transformations yet to come." The visit of his father to the cottage where he and Claire are spending their summer of contentment, not only brings him hints of death, it also takes away his sexual power. David suddenly feels robbed of his desire, and he describes himself as the victim-hero of the Gogol story who is mortified to discover that his nose has been stolen. Just as the Gogal character runs to the newspaper office to place a classified ad seeking the return of his nose, Roth's narrator thinks of rushing to his psychiatrist to find his lost desire. David Kepish now describes himself as "the butt of a ridiculous, vicious inexplicable joke!" The final joke, however, is not that he has lost his desire, but rather the bizarre form of its return. The professor of literature who has read too much Chekhov and Gogal and Kafka will soon metamorphose into a giant version of the breast which he sucks upon at the end of the novel. He will become mistress, mother, and Eve all at once.

No other novelist of the 1970s has been quite as bold when it comes to turning a narrator into a victim-hero. The success of Roth's novel depends upon the scope of the narrator's voice—the ability of David Kepesh as a professor of literature to find mirrors from Chekhov to Kafka. But the use of such mirrors in the fiction of Roth suggests the endless interface of life and art. If it is the fate of David Kepesh to actually become the reflection of his own forbidden desire, what

happens to readers of Chekhov, Kafka, and Roth? "It is now life and
not art," Lionel Trilling has suggested, "that requires the willing
suspension of disbelief."

Notes

[1] John Enck, "John Barth: An Interview," *Wisconsin Studies in Contemporary Literature*, 6 (Winter-Spring 1965), p. 11.

[2] Interview with Saul Bellow in "The Act of Fiction, XXXVII," *The Paris Review*, 9 (Winter 1966), 61.

[3] Sara Davidson, "Talk with Philip Roth," *New York Times Book Review*, September 18, 1977, p. 51.

[4] *Chicago Tribune Book World*, October 23, 1977, p. 2, and Allen Lacy, "A Hint of Nightmare Amid Innocence," *Chronicle of Higher Education*, October 25, 1977, p. 16.

[5] Ihab Hassan, *Radical Innocence: Studies in the Contemporary American Novel* (Princeton: Princeton University Press, 1961), pp. 69-70.

[6] Philip Roth, *The Professor of Desire* (New York: Farrar, Straus and Giroux, 1977), p. 9. All further references to this edition are cited parenthetically.

[7] Philip Roth, *Reading Myself and Others* (New York: Bantam Books, 1977), p. 78.

[8] Franz Kafka, *Letter to his Father*, translated by Ernest Kaiser and Eithe Wilkins (New York: Shocken Books, 1953), p. 87.

1978

Gore Vidal
Kalki

Gore Vidal was in his early twenties with three novels to his credit when he visited George Santayana in the hospital of the Convent of the Blue Nuns in Rome. At their parting, the young novelist received "a benediction laid on with the left hand" from the aged philosopher. Years later Vidal could still recall Santayana's last words to him: "I think you will have a happy life. Because you lack superstition."[1] In more than thirty volumes—stories, novels, plays, and essays—Gore Vidal has been faithful to Santayana's prophecy. He has exposed and ridiculed the power of superstition from the early spread of Christianity to the destructive force of various religious cults today. In each of the last three decades of Vidal's career, one novel stands out for its satire of religious superstition. In the 1950s Vidal published *Messiah* which mocks Christianity with the success of a death-worshipping cult; in the 1960s he published *Julian* which dramatizes the intelligence of Greece and Rome challenged by the dark power of Christian dogma; and in 1978 he published *Kalki* which depicts the end of the world achieved by a self-proclaimed savior-destroyer. The dying American philosopher in the convent of the Blue Nuns was a more accurate prophet than either he or his young guest could possibly have suspected.

Vidal's imaginative ridicule of superstition has not gone unnoticed—*Julian* and *Kalki* were best-sellers—but the academic reviewers of literature have been slow to recognize the merit of Vidal's fiction. If his books are so popular, how can they be any good? Vidal also has done much to maintain his adversary relationship with the critics he likes to dismiss as "the hacks of academe." In his own critical essays he has mocked the funeral directors of literature: "The new critics had laid it out all neat in a blue suit, a flower in its waxy hands (HERE LIES THE NOVEL, EXPLICATED), and their funeral orations were already under way in the literary quarterlies."[2] Nor have the more recent followers of French theories about the new-novel, structuralism, semiology, etc. escaped Vidal's sarcastic wit. If they are not guilty of "the slow killing of the work through a close textual analysis," Vidal exposes their critical dogmas and concludes that such "teachers of English are the new barbarians, serenely restoring the Dark Ages."[3] True believers in the work of Barthes and Derrida are ridiculed as victims of the French Pox. Small wonder that Vidal's work remains largely unsung and unknown by the academic guardians of literary value.

Recently, signs of a truce have begun to emerge on both sides. A few academic monographs on the work of Vidal have been published. The first to appear was a volume for the Twayne series on American authors. Vidal himself wrote a favorable review for *The New York Times.* "A most interesting book," wrote Gore Vidal about *Gore Vidal,* "astonishingly exact in detail and often shrewd in judgment."[4] Other critical monographs have followed, and no doubt a few graduate students are now hard at work on dissertations comparing the Wife of Bath and Myra Breckinridge. The ultimate revenge of the academy will be to make Vidal's work respectable. In recent years Vidal, with frequent essays in *The New York Review of Books* and a well publicized tour of American campuses, has done his share to occupy the enemy territory. Sooner or later the truce was inevitable. Vidal will be burdened before long with honorary degrees, and the return of the prodigal will be complete.

The self-reflexive design of all three Vidal novels which dramatize his satire of religious superstition should be of most interest to critics exploring the techniques of Post-Modernism. Santayana would have been pleased to see how Vidal has developed the strategy of unfolding the story of a novel within the memoirs of a skeptical narrator. *Messiah* is presented as the memoir of a dying man long considered a heretic by the cult of death-worshippers he once helped to establish. The design of *Julian* is even more complex. The fictional memoir of the Emperor, himself the most powerful skeptic of the early Christian dogmas, is framed by the editorial comments of two of Julian's contemporaries who reflect upon his memoir with the varying degrees of their own skepticism. The structure of the novel thus resembles a triple mirror in which each image can be cast back at different angles. The fictions of Borges, Barthe, and Barthelme all play with the same self-reflexive principle, but Vidal does not indulge the practice of mirror images simply for its own sake. He has long felt at home in the comic house of mirrors, and has skillfully been able to adapt the style of multiple reflection to depict complex historical subjects. The diversification of viewpoint in his trilogy on American history—*Washington, D.C., Burr,* and *1876*—owes much to his experimentation with mirror images in *Julian.*

Not only are the views of Julian reflected by two of his contemporaries who tend to agree with his opposition to Christianity, but the image of the Emperor is also presented in the novel as a possible likeness of the very behavior he opposes. The most skeptical and cynical voice in the novel labels Julian as a "Christian mystic gone wrong." The more Julian opposes the spread of Christian dogma, the more superstitious and dogmatic his own beliefs become. The ironic resemblance of the apostate and the image of the faith he challenges is a predictable result of the design of mirrors. Melville demonstrates the same principle in *Moby-Dick* when he matches the terrible vengeance of Ahab to the image of "eternal malice" that he attacks. Not only does Ahab's irrational fury increase as he prepares to strike through the mask at his deadly foe, even his ship with its bulwarks "garnished like one continuous jaw" is a mirror image of its prey. "He who fights with monsters," Nietzsche later wrote, "should be careful lest he thereby become a monster." Melville and Vidal leave no doubt about the danger and power of mirror images. If it is fair to credit Melville with anticipating the self-reflexive concerns of recent fiction, it is possible to see in the novels of Gore Vidal how the contemporary interest in mirror images has been developed into full religious satire.

Vidal's latest and best attack on religious superstition is *Kalki,* a remarkable novel which dramatizes the sudden death of four billion people. The end of the human race is arranged by a pleasant American, Jim Kelly, who may or may not be the tenth and final avatar of Vishnu. He was an expert on bacteriological warfare in Vietnam, who disappeared after the "peace with honor," and then emerged in Katmandu as a self-proclaimed incarnation of the Hindu deity. Throughout the novel Vidal keeps the reader in suspense about Kelly's true nature. Is he a very successful operator conducting international drug traffic behind the shield of a growing religious cult? Is he a hustler of sham mysticism expecting to make money from his disciples who are increasing worldwide? Or is he the final avatar of Vishnu foretold in the Hindu writings? Kalki and Siva are names of the deity expected to take human form when it is time for the end of the present world. Beyond the destruction of this life, Kalki is supposed to create a new age. The anticipation of a golden time by devout Hindus is analogous to the millennial expectation of Christians. Vidal takes delight in mocking such metaphysical dreams. When human life is extinguished in *Kalki*, the world is taken over by chattering monkeys.

The novel is presented to us in the form of a memoir by the last survivors of the human race. Five men and women have been inoculated against the bacteria which has been spread around the globe to eliminate the other four billion people. The five include Jim Kelly, the self-proclaimed avatar of Vishnu, his second wife known as Lakshmi or the Queen of Heaven, her friend Geraldine whose research in genetics at MIT could be helpful in creating new forms of life, Giles Lowell, the ultimate double agent of the novel, and Teddy Ottinger, a famous pilot who serves as Vidal's principal narrator.

In the earlier novels which satirize religious superstition, *Messiah* and *Julian*, the narrative device of a fictitious memoir is used to form a series of ironic mirrors. A similar strategy is revealed in *Kalki*. The narrator once again is a skeptical companion of the self-proclaimed god. This time, however, the narrator does witness the fulfillment of several incredible prophecies. Indeed, it is Teddy Ottinger who completes two flights around the globe in order to distribute, without knowing it, the fatal bacteria. The story is told in retrospect by this narrator who is trying to understand her role in the end of the human race, her relationship to Kalki, and her responsibility to the age waiting to be born.

Who is Vidal's narrator? She has been married, the mother of two children, and recently divorced. She pays alimony to her husband who keeps the children, while she pursues a career as a pilot and journalist. Vidal's satire of the women's liberation movement is merely one example of how the cultural roots of this novel grow from the 1970s. Teddy Ottinger is also the author of a best-selling book called *Beyond Motherhood*. It is the story of her liberation from marriage and childbearing. Unfortunately her book was ghostwritten

by an untalented hack named Herman Victor Weiss. Teddy is haunted
by the sensibility of this writer, and often struggles to find her own
words apart from the clichés she knows would be typical of Weiss. She
must find her own words as the narrator of *Kalki*, because all of the
ghostwriters in the world have become ghosts. This information,
however, is kept from us until late in the novel. At first we are told that
the narrator is in the White House writing her report; gradually we
learn of the extraordinary events that have brought her to this position. She attempts to avoid hindsight, and merely describe the events
of the year as she experienced them. The result is a narrative of
considerable suspense in which realistic detail and fantastic happen-
ings form a comic satire of the credulous, decadent, and dead 1970s.

Vidal's narrator is a cynical, pragmatic, and self-professed
atheist. She only goes to Katmandu as a journalist to interview the
American who claims to be a Hindu deity. She finds Jim Kelly to be
a handsome young man, and she welcomes his passion despite her
sexual preference for older women. Perhaps she cannot resist sleeping
with a god. His promises, in any event, are remarkable:

> I am the ultimate avatar, the last incarnation within this
> cycle of time. On the day that I mount the white horse, the
> sword Nandaka blazing like a comet in my right hand, I
> shall destroy the wicked. At my approach the flesh of this
> world will fall away like grass before the scythe, and the
> age of Kali will be no more. Then, in the stillness of the
> void, I shall re-create the human race. The golden age will
> come again. For I am Kalki. I am Vishnu. I am the highest
> of the high.[5]

At first Teddy responds to the Hindu rhetoric with complete disbelief—"I was entirely skeptical." She remains convinced that "most
religions are rackets," but the physical charms of the self-proclaimed
avatar of Vishnu are undeniable—"I was also entirely attracted to Mr.
Kelly." While she tries to deny the god and accept the man, her
skepticism will be constantly under attack. The comedy of Vidal's
novel depends on making the outrageous claims of the self-styled god
seem to come true before the eyes of the skeptical narrator.

The narrator's appraisal of what happens is most important
because all of the events in the novel are only available to us through
her memory. At each stage of her account Teddy remains uncertain

about the true nature of her companions. Although an obtuse narrator is hardly new in the history of fiction, the uncertainty principle (Heisenberg or Vidal) is honored with greater frequency in contemporary fiction. The narrator is part of the world she observes and, therefore, can never be objectively certain about the nature of what is happening. Vidal takes this principle to the limits of dramatic absurdity when he has his narrator blindly drop poison on four billion people. Teddy only learns after the event that she has been effectively responsible for the end of the world's population. At the time she was merely doing her job as a reliable pilot for Kalki Enterprises. The important question—for whom does Kalki work?—remains throughout the novel. Vidal's narrator cannot reach a final answer, but it is not for any lack of skill or persistence. Teddy is intelligent and perceptive. Her role as a journalist requires her to discover the truth about Kalki. The novel often reads like a detective fiction with the narrator trying to unmask the identities of the various double and triple agents. Nevertheless, the principle of uncertainty rules at the heart of the matter, and the pursuit of truth merely leads the narrator further into the house of mirrors.

Although she is not at all religious, Teddy does have a talent for metaphysical speculation. She recalls with vain satisfaction how she won a debate in college with the head of the French Department at USC. The subject was Descartes, and Teddy argued for the necessary failure of any attempt to establish a causal proof for the existence of a god. Her skepticism will later become the perfect foil to the mystical rhetoric of Kalki. Teddy would have become a graduate student in philosophy at USC if only the registration lines had not been so long. Instead, she becomes a journalist, and is sent to Katmandu to interview the self-proclaimed Hindu god. Her talent for rational argument and analysis is severely tried when she finds herself in the uncertain world of Hindu mysticism. Shadow and substance are interchangeable at the center of Kalki's international religious cult, and the uncertainty principle reigns supreme.

Vidal's narrator retains her skepticism through the interview in Katmandu. Later she questions herself—"Did I take any of this seriously at the time?"—and answers with a firm "No." After she hears the promises of Kalki, Teddy concludes: "I thought he was either mad or a great actor, or both." Her skepticism is reinforced by a conversation with Kelly's first wife who scoffs at the idea of her recent husband becoming a god: "I've never read such nonsense. Ever! How a good Catholic boy like Jimmy could end up spouting all this Hindu non-sense is beyond me.... He's up to something. But I don't know what" (104).

It is Teddy's job to find out what Kalki is up to. His wild promises have begun to attract world-wide attention. Comedians on television have started to joke nervously about "The End." Mike Wallace has even traveled to Katmandu to interview Kalki for his news program. Vidal takes delight in satirizing the creation of news for the television audience. Kalki may or may not be the final avatar of Vishnu, but he certainly knows how to attract the media.

The publicity campaign for Kalki Enterprises focuses all expectation upon a rally to be held at Madison Square Garden. It proves to be a theatrical extravaganza watched by millions on television who believe they see Kalki and his white horse explode into bits. Even those present at the Garden prefer to watch the event on TV screens. "This was a commonplace in that era," remarks Teddy, "events were only real if experienced at second hand, preferably through the medium of the camera." Such "reality" is deceptive; twenty pages later Kalki walks back into the novel as alive as ever. His "resurrection," of course, scores another media sensation, and he is interviewed by "the greatest pitchperson on television." The full comedy of the scene depends on Vidal bringing together the high priestess of television commercials, where all problems may be eliminated by the miracles of a consumer society, and the self-proclaimed Hindu god who is pre-pared to announce the consummation of the world. It is during this interview that Kalki sets the date for the death of all people. "That is not really a very upbeat sort of message," replies the voice of commercial America. Even when Kalki explains that death is "the ultimate blessing," the common and naive voice of the TV announcer continues to ask for "a message of hope." Nothing, however, in Vidal's novel spells relief. When the date for the end of the world is announced, it is calmly reported by Walter Cronkite with only a slight lifting of one eyebrow. When the self-proclaimed Siva begins the dance of eternity, Vidal's narrator reports in a matter-of-fact tone that the world "came to its predicted end."

Neither the sudden death of four billion people, nor the mere survival of Kalki and his four inoculated companions, alters the realistic tone of the novel. Despite the outrageous premise of the book,

Vidal is not interested in science fiction or the typical effects of a horror story. Instead, the narrator retains the tone of trying to explain the incredible events in a rational manner. The uncertainty of human nature and the appeal of religious superstition remain Vidal's subjects for analysis and satire.

In the twilight period after the kiss of Siva has been delivered to the world, Teddy Ottinger still questions the identity of her companions: "I don't know who Kalki is. Beyond being a mass murderer." Such doubts sound like heresy to Geraldine who points to the dead world and claims with pride: "This is the work of Vishnu. And no one else" (229). What can the skeptical narrator believe? She remains unconvinced: "I chose not to judge."

How does Vidal expect his audience to respond? Can the novel be read with the willing suspension of disbelief normally allowed a work of fiction in which events are described in a matter-of-fact tone? Other novelists of the 1970s, especially Heller and Doctorow, have played with the conventions of realism by mixing historical figures with fully invented characters. When Vidal places Walter Cronkite and Kalki in the same novel, the fictional character seems more credible, the historical figure suddenly turned into a fiction. Early in the novel the narrator is greeted by Merv Griffin next to the pool of the Beverly Hills Hotel. Vidal's ability to fix his novel in a contemporary setting helps to convince us that later events, however implausible, may still take place in a world where TV personalities are omnipresent. Such a world is ready for the revelations of Kalki.

Vidal's novel, however, challenges the standards of literary realism on another level. Ordinarily a reader is able to suspend disbelief in the events of a novel despite their fantastic nature if the events are described in a plausible and realistic manner. But how does a reader respond if he happens to come to the novel already possessing some of the beliefs that are being satirized? More than five hundred million Hindus are alive today who officially believe that the final avatar of Vishnu will come to end this cycle of the world. Nine hundred million Christians have been taught to expect the similar return of Christ and the advent of the milennium. For these people, reading the novel would not be an experience so much of suspending disbelief as of distinguishing their own beliefs from Vidal's mockery. What is enjoyed in the novel by some as religious satire will be regarded by others as blasphemy. Like the narrators of *Messiah* and

Julian who take delight in baiting Christians, the narrator of *Kalki* describes her fan mail: "Most of it was from fundamentalist Christians who were praying for me as they stitched their hoods, lit their crosses, planned pogroms." Perhaps all novels select their readers, and true believers will be safe from the wit and sarcasm of Vidal's satire. In any event, Santayana's left-handed benediction was delivered in the doorway of the Convent of the Blue Nuns.

Vidal's satire of religious superstition is appropriately set in the late 1970s. The president of the United States until the day Siva begins the dance of eternity is described as "a twice-born redneck from the South." The governor of California is identified as "a Zen Buddhist who slept on the floor." In an essay on the state of American culture published a few years before the novel, Vidal concludes: "this generation of Americans is god-hungry and craves reassurance of personal immortality."[6] This view is not only dramatized in *Kalki* by the enormous success of the self-proclaimed Hindu messiah, but also by the many references to other religious confidence men and the wide variety of panaceas available to contemporary Americans. The targets of Vidal's satire include Christian Science, E.S.T., Scientology, and the evangelical empire of the Reverend Moon.

Religious and political corruption are often linked in Vidal's picture of contemporary decadence: "The Reverend Sun Moon was thought to be paid for by the government of South Korea which was paid for by the American Congress whose members, in turn, were given kickbacks by the South Koreans" (32). Speculation about bribery is prevalent in the novel. One character is rumored to be a quadruple agent: working simultaneously for a Republican senator who wants to be president, a drug syndicate in Asia, the CIA in Washington, and finally as a part-time murderer for Kalki Enterprises. Small wonder that the narrator has difficulty assigning identity to the various characters.

Vidal is especially good at satirizing the final stages of a dying culture. The library of one character in the novel consists entirely of a leatherbound complete set of *TV Guide*. Twenty thousand billboards across America have been paid for by Kalki Enterprises to announce "The End." The novel even includes the final newscast of Walter Cronkite: "And that's the way it is, Monday April 2. . . ." The next day Jim Kelly appears as Siva and begins the dance of eternity. Except for the religious zealots who are born again into a variety of contradictory faiths, the inhabitants of the novel appear to drift in mindless circles. Drugs, smog, and television are pervasive. In or out of the religious sects the mood is one of waiting for the end. Yeats' vision of anarchy in "The Second Coming" is a preview of the situation in Vidal's novel: "Things fall apart; the centre cannot hold. . . . The best lack all conviction, while the worst/Are full of passionate intensity." Many of Vidal's characters are waiting for the rough beast, or any beast at all, to begin slouching towards Bethlehem.

The crowds of dazed citizens are capable of distinguishing neither among the commercial claims made incessantly on television nor among the supernatural claims made by the many religious charlatans. Consequently, the forms of relief, the desperate panaceas, and the bizarre faiths keep multiplying. Illusion and reality are interchangeable in this world of television mirrors. The narrator lives with a star of countless TV commercials, and the resulting confusion is typical of the world Vidal is satirizing: "There is a sense of unreality, of double exposure living with someone whose face you have seen all your life on television . . . inner and outer grow confused, blur." Vidal is interested in how the standards of a television culture have affected the conventions of literary realism. The images reflected in his novel may seem real to contemporary readers because they resemble the fictions that pass for news on the TV screen. The final twist of satire is to have Walter Cronkite announce that Kalki will begin the dance of eternity. Cronkite? Kalki? Vidal? Who is the ultimate confidence man?

If games of illusion are characteristic of the post-modern novel, *Kalki* is certainly no exception. Although the narrator has studied Descartes, her training in philosophy does not enable her to distinguish reality from fiction in the metaphysical world of *Kalki*. Uncertainty prevails when the inner and outer grow confused and blur. The narrator's two male companions, Giles Lowell and Jim Kelly, provide the most intricate puzzles of identity. Teddy first meets Lowell on the plane en route to Katmandu. He introduces himself as Dr. Ashok, a native of India and a devout Hindu, and he claims to be headed for Nepal in order to expose the false designs of Kalki. Vidal's narrator is immediately suspicious; she thinks perhaps that Dr. Ashok is an agent of the CIA but abandons this theory as soon as he produces CIA identification. In a world of disguises, all evidence is counterproductive. The narrator only feels certain that her mysterious traveling companion "radiated treachery." Later, the disguise of Dr. Ashok is cast aside, and the character of Giles Lowell emerges. He is the mastermind who plans the worldwide campaign of Kalki, and after the murder of four billion people, he is the one who challenges Kalki for control of the golden age. Lowell is the devil figure of the novel, the ultimate double agent, whose pride forces him to challenge the authority of a god. Like the devil, Lowell or Ashok is everywhere in the novel. Wearing the disguise of one character, he may even criticize the other. The narrator is rightly suspicious, but she cannot hope to penetrate the disguises of the archetypal confidence man. Near the end of the novel, the true identity of this double character is questioned: "'I wonder who you really are. I mean, deep down inside. Is Dr. Lowell impersonating Dr. Ashok or does Dr. Ashok impersonate Dr. Lowell?' 'A true mystery. . . . Personally, I suspect that each is really the other and neither one is me'" (255). Asking the devil to explain himself has never proved very helpful, but the devil is only the shadow of a god—the true mystery of the novel is the nature of Kalki.

In many of his essays Vidal has explained "there is no reality for man except in his relations with his own kind," and "the order of the universe is, finally, inscrutable."[7] The narrator of *Kalki* echoes the same point of view early in the novel when she proclaims, "I like only what is demonstrable." The remarkable performance of Kalki may test her skepticism but not remove her uncertainty. The play of illusion and reality is continuous in a mind which tries to imagine the interchange of men and gods in cycles of creation and destruction.

After the annihilation of all but five people, the most extraordinary scenes of the novel unfold. The empty world is only briefly enjoyed by the few survivors. The animals soon begin to inherit the ruins of man. Lions can be observed moving near the White House, and giraffes are visible on the lawn of Mount Vernon. Kalki and his wife expect to repopulate the world with their offspring, but their first and only child is born dead and deformed. The golden age will be left to the monkeys which have been adopted by the narrator and ironically treated as children by a woman who is famous for being "beyond-motherhood." Her last paragraph describes the inheritors of the golden age: "Bright red birds on the wing. Silver fish that briefly arc above the surface of a river which glitters in the sun like a silver fish's scales" (272). Her last words in the novel refer to the monkey cradled in her lap as "The Child."

The next and final journal entry in the novel is made sixteen years after the death of Teddy Ottinger. The only survivor now is Kalki. For the first and last time in the novel his words come to us directly without quotation marks. The subject is self-revelation:

> I am breath. I am spirit. I am the supreme lord. I alone was before all things, and I exist and I shall be. No other transcends me. I am eternal and not eternal, discernible and undiscernible. I am Brahma and I am not Brahma. I am without beginning, middle or end. At the time of the end, I annihilate all worlds.
> I am Siva. (273-274)

The novel ends with this religious ego trip characteristic of the paradoxes of illusion and reality Vidal has been playing with all along.

The words of Kalki or Brahma or Siva leave us with the same confusion that Teddy Ottinger has confronted throughout the novel. The existence of any god is doubted by Vidal's narrator. The existence of three gods in one strikes her as particularly absurd. Despite her study of Hindu mysticism undertaken before her first interview with Jim Kelly, the multiple names of the Hindu deity never make sense to her. If all gods are understood to be the inventions of human fears and hopes, then the multiplicity of gods is a basic reflection of the uncertainty and diversity of nature. For this very principle Julian lives and dies in Vidal's earlier novel: "Every god and goddess known to the people, no matter in what guise or under what strange name, would be worshipped, for multiplicity is the nature of life."[8] Julian fights a losing battle against the narrowness, the dogma, the limiting piety of the Christians. He warns them in vain that "the greatness of our world was the gift of other gods and a different, more subtle philosophy, reflecting the variety in nature." With the death of the Emperor Julian nothing is left to halt the spread of Christianity, and Vidal concludes that novel with the dark ages descending upon the world. The record of the immediate future in *Kalki* reaches an even darker conclusion. The incantation of the man-god at the end of the novel is the only voice remaining in a dead world.

Vidal's satire of religious superstition thus comes in the form of a dark prophecy. He goes beyond Orwell and Huxley to show how millennial expectations may cancel the future. There is a moment in the novel when the protagonist hears the different voices in his head, and almost understands the tragedy: "Sometimes the whispers in my head tell me that symmetry may require the absolute end of this race in time. Strange, isn't it? Siva whispers, annihilate man. Vishnu whispers, preserve. Brahma whispers, begin a new cycle. Is there any beer?' (243). The unexpected last question comes from the earthly voice of Jim Kelly, but the natural man is lost when the voices of god begin to whisper in his head, and among the different aspects of god the voice of Siva is the most powerful. The final appeal of religious superstition is an ultimate death wish, and Vidal therefore concludes his satire with the all-destructive voice of Siva.

Notes

[1] Vidal's account of Santayana, *Rocking the Boat* (Boston: Little, Brown, 1962), pp. xi-xii.

[2] Gore Vidal, *Homage to Daniel Shays, Collected Essays 1952-1972* (New York: Random House, 1972), p. 28.

[3] Gore Vidal, *Matters of Fact and Fiction, Essays 1973-1976* (New York: Random House, 1977), p. 114.

[4] *New York Times Book Review*, September 1, 1968, rpt. in Gore Vidal, *Reflections Upon a Sinking Ship* (Boston: Little, Brown, 1968), p. 231.

[5] Gore Vidal, *Kalki* (New York: Random House, 1978), p. 60. All further references to this edition are cited parenthetically.

[6] *Matters of Fact and Fiction*, p. 122.

[7] *Rocking the Boat*, p. 137.

[8] Gore Vidal, *Julian* (Boston: Little, Brown, 1964), p. 329.

1979

Joseph Heller
Good as Gold

No other first novel by an American in this century has attracted as much commentary as Joseph Heller's *Catch-22*. Within two months of its publication in 1961 reviewers were already confident that the novel would "become a classic."[1] The launching of Heller's book into the public consciousness is now a legend among publishers, and for students of American literature it may suggest how a contemporary "classic" is promoted, reviewed, and cannonized.

Although early reviews of *Catch-22* were often mixed in judgment, a competition soon appeared to see who could praise the novel in the most extravagant terms. The prize belongs to W. J. Miller: "Properly appreciated, *Catch-22* finally impresses the reader as being a great artistic statement of man's condition comparable to Homer's *Iliad*, Dante's *Inferno*, or Joyce's *Finnegans Wake*."[2] Not bad for a first novel! The debased currency of literary criticism no doubt amused the novelist who had long worked as an advertising writer in New York. Whatever the dubious value of the many literary judgments made about *Catch-22*, Joseph Heller knew that all of the publicity would be as good as gold.

In the dozen years after *Catch-22* more than six books and five hundred articles or reviews were devoted to commentary and analysis of the novel. Reading through much of the commentary is not likely to convince anyone of the subtlety and depth of recent literary discussion. Critics of all persuasions have ridden their hobby horses into the inviting fields of the novel. Psychologists have found angst and schizophrenia. Sociologists have discovered alienation and the perils of bureaucracy. Philosophers have identified seven types of existentialism. After such knowledge what forgiveness? Debating the worth of various labels has been the most common critical approach. Should the novel be classified as an example of black humor, a vision of the absurd, a surrealistic satire, or a military cartoon? Why not all of the above? Critics have also pondered at great length whether the main character is the only sane man in a mad world or vice versa. Their decision is eagerly awaited. Enough has been written about the "surrealistic" aspects of Milo Minderbinder to make one wonder if the character has not been able to market his famous chocolate covered cotton as literary criticism.

The extraordinary success of his first book generated unusual interest about the next novel that Heller was known to be writing. The public, however, was kept waiting. After five years a two page preview of the unfinished work appeared in *Esquire* with the title "Something Happened." But not much happened. Another eight years would pass before the novel itself was actually published. Book clubs had been ready for a decade to schedule the novel as a featured selection. Who knows how many publicity agents passed away during the extended drum roll for the appearance of *Something Happened*.

The novel was quickly reviewed in almost two hundred publications. Some shock and dismay was initially reported when reviewers looked in vain for the humor and vitality that had been so characteristic of *Catch-22*, but only a few early warnings were sounded about the dismal qualities of the new book. If it had not been for the fame of the author and the great expectations of the public, this monumental bore of a novel would have been allowed to lumber off unnoticed to the elephant burial ground. Instead, in one review after another, heroic efforts were made to breathe life into the inert hulk. All of its defects were paraded forth as virtues. If the novel seemed dull, it was described as a true picture of dull reality. If the novel appeared repetitious and simpleminded, it was defended as a realistic drama of life's meaninglessness. If the novel seemed pointless and absurd, its apologists argued that absurdity was its point. The appearance of *Something Happened* was an irresistible moment for reviewers to express their moral and social concerns about the human condition. Will literary criticism ever be free of such crying in the desert? The rhetoric of John Aldridge in *Saturday Review World* may illustrate the genre: "But to humanize a condition in which dehumanization is not merely the primary fact of life but the primary subject of consciousness is a nearly miraculous artistic feat."[3] The miracle, needless to say, was only visible to the true believers. Experience gradually triumphed over expectations, and *Something Happened* has neither enjoyed the continued sales nor the growing acceptance of *Catch-22*.

Joseph Heller clearly could not afford to let another thirteen years pass before the appearance of his next book. Nor could he risk another very long novel. His reputation as a comic writer could only be saved by returning to some of the tricks that had worked in *Catch-22*. Is there a rule in American literature that third novels tend to be the best? It was true with the career of F. Scott Fitzgerald, and it now appears to be the case with Joseph Heller. *Good as Gold* is a major step forward in Heller's career. The novel combines many of the virtues of his first two books while avoiding most of their faults. If *Catch-22* and *Something Happened* are both repetitive and rambling in structure, *Good as Gold* is unified and coherent. If the first two novels tend to indulge a sense of humor that is often sophomoric, the third book reveals a steady wit that is fully integrated with character and situation. Heller's skill at the craft of fiction has made clear advances in characterization, narrative control, and most of all in dramatic timing.

Good as Gold is a mixture of three different kinds of fiction: a Jewish family novel, a political satire, and the story of superman demythologized. The protagonist, Bruce Gold, is the focal point for all three. He is the youngest son in a large Jewish family. He is tempted by the vague promise of a high political office in Washington. And he is greatly annoyed by the bold success of Henry Kissinger in the role of superman. Is it possible for any Jewish professor, Bruce Gold asks himself, to suddenly emerge from a telephone booth as Secretary of State? It is his comic predicament to want, receive, and scorn the call to Washington.

It should not be a complete surprise to find Heller writing a Jewish family novel. It is true that Yossarian in *Catch-22* is neither Jewish nor connected with a family, but in an early sketch for the novel, before Heller decided to make his hero "outside culture in every way—ethnically as well as others," Yossarian was identified as a Jew.[4] It is also true that the hero in *Something Happened* is described as a suburban WASP, but at least one reviewer for the *Jewish Times* saw the novel differently: "The people are supposed to be Christian but Heller isn't fooling anybody."[5] What may have been suppressed in the first two novels is totally explicit in the third. Not only is the title character of Heller's third novel fully dramatized among his Jewish family and friends, he is even writing a book about "the Jewish experience." The book that Bruce Gold has agreed to write may be viewed as the very novel that his fictional presence dominates. His experience as a Jew, loved and trapped by his large family, tempted and frustrated by the myth of Kissinger, is the drama of *Good as Gold*.

How does Joseph Heller expect to capture the territory of fiction so often held by Philip Roth and Saul Bellow? American literature is hardly suffering from a shortage of authors ready to dramatize "the Jewish experience." Heller recognizes the competition, and succeeds by turning the conventional genre into a comic parody. If the typical Jewish protagonist often feels threatened by the anxious counsel of his immediate family, the hero of Heller's novel is inundated by the contradictory advice of no less than fifteen close relatives. If the family meal is supposed to be a ritual of the passover feast, the dinners of the Gold family rival the banquets in the *Satyricon* for headache and heartburn. If the heroes of Roth and Bellow often seem to live in a world invented by Kafka, the protagonist of *Good as Gold* is haunted by shadows of persecution that even appear as messages in his Chinese fortune cookies. Heller is especially good when it comes to pushing conventional themes to absurd limits. Portnoy may work for the Mayor of New York, but Bruce Gold will be summoned to Washington to meet President Carter. Herzog may drift from Madeleine to Ramona, but Gold is married to Belle, engaged to Andrea, and in love with Linda, all at the same time. Much of Heller's comedy depends upon outrageous multiplication.

The size of Gold's family and their mixture of concern and mockery for him inspire many of the comic scenes in the novel. Heller creates five sisters and a brother all with their respective mates and suitors. Small wonder that Gold considers family parties "grueling and monotonous tests of fealty to which he submitted with sorrow and anxiety whenever he was left with no civilized alternative."[6] The novel is punctuated with such parties at which Gold is admired and teased as the family intellectual. The fact that he teaches at a university and writes books is a source of wonder and amusement to his relatives. With the best intentions his sisters defend him by reminding one another: "There's no need to be ashamed of him just because he writes things nobody understands." Gold does not know how to accept their pride and love especially when it takes the form of comic mockery. His brother Sid is particularly adept at leading Gold into conversations that will abandon him in nonsense. The dialogues about blind vultures and why rivers flow downhill are among the great comic moments in the book. Gold's advanced degree in English literature and his professional reputation as the author of six books offer no defense when his brother Sid begins to talk about blind vultures. All the family parties serve to wreck the nerves of the hero who cannot understand how his relatives are having such a good time. Blind fury, comic impotence, sullen restraint, none of the responses of Gold can save him from the torment of his relatives.

The headache of family conversation is only surpassed by the heartburn caused by the extraordinary meals. All of the sisters multiply the available dishes at every gathering. The competition of Belle's potato kugel and Muriel's "monstrous scarlet meatloaf" burdens Gold with all of the rewards of gluttony. When the conversation becomes especially frustrating Gold will often try to lose himself in the noodle pudding. The culinary adventures of the Jewish family in Heller's novel turn *Good as Gold* into a comic feast.

Despite the size of his family and the abundance of their food, the bedeviled hero of the novel never feels at home. Heller knows how the ghost of Franz Kafka haunts contemporary Jewish fiction, and thus he multiplies the homeless insecurity of his protagonist until it assumes comic proportions. Gold often feels that his whole family has joined together to form a conspiracy against him. Worse yet, he feels that the rest of the world also stands ready to make fun of him. Although he scorns his family and friends, he suffers constantly from what he imagines they must think of him. Heller is very skillful at exploiting the comic potential of Gold's insecurity. After a dinner at a Chinese restaurant with his contentious family, while they all receive the typical messages from fortune cookies, Gold is confounded to read his fate: "You will hurt your foot." Everyone, except Gold, thinks that it is very amusing.

Heller also adds to his comic design by imposing some very difficult parents upon his hapless protagonist. Instead of the sympathetic father that Philip Roth gives to his hero in *The Professor of Desire*, Joseph Heller provides his fictional professor with a "demanding, autocratic old four-flusher of a father," who never wastes an opportunity to criticize his son. "It was no secret to anyone that his father

considered Gold a *schmuck*" (24). Instead of the worried and posses-
sive mother familiar in *Portnoy's Complaint*, Heller creates an insane
stepmother who likes to observe that the screws in Gold's head are
coming loose. Playing variations against the parents expected in
novels of Jewish family life allows Heller to explore new comic
territory. The insane stepmother is forever knitting a shroud of white
wool, and Gold is promised that someday it will fit on one of his feet.
The impossible father delays leaving for his usual winter in Florida,
and discovers instead new Jewish holidays which the family must
celebrate together. Plagued by parents like this, Gold at times resembles a parody of Job.

Heller also multiplies the comic troubles of his hero by dou-
bling and tripling the number of women in his romantic imagination.
The dreams of Portnoy and Herzog are developed further in the
bemused philanderings of Gold. Appointment to a high position in
Washington, he is told, will depend upon his marriage to the tall,
attractive daughter of a very rich anti-Semite. Her vision of sex
includes "whips and costumes and riding crops," but her most remarkable offer of submission is much in keeping with the comic leitmotiv
of the novel—"I can eat your foot." That is not exactly Gold's idea of
sensual pleasure, but if political success demands it, then he is ready.
Soon he is engaged to the willowy masochist, but a final separation
from his wife and her potato kugel will not be easy. "We have death
sometimes," says his autocratic father, "but no divorces" (114). While
commuting between his two women, Gold typically falls in love with
a third. That she happens to be his daughter's teacher, and happens
also to possess a husband and four children, is characteristic of
Heller's strategy of multiplying the comic potential. Now the dreams
of Gold can dramatize the favors of all three women. He plans a trip
to Acapulco, where he expects to have his fiancée and his mistress, not
to mention a separate room for himself to catch his breath between the
rounds of pleasure. Gold never does get to Acapulco, but one of the
great scenes of the novel is his fantasy of trying to please the two
women in the adjoining hotel rooms. Even his fantasy proves so
exhausting that Gold collapses and has to be taken to the hospital,
where for ten days neither mistress, fiancée, nor wife, miss him at all.
Heller's ability to mine comic gold in the veins of Roth and Bellow
adds a new chapter to the fiction of "the Jewish experience" in
American literature.

The second genre of fiction that is explored by Heller in *Good as Gold* is political satire. Although many of the Washington scenes are not among the best in the novel, they still afford Heller the chance to ridicule the bureaucracy in ways that are reminiscent of the satire in *Catch-22*. Gold's appetite for sex and food and money is only surpassed by his ambition for a high post in Washington. It is not really power that Gold desires, but rather the respect of all the people who are prone to make fun of him. His family and friends will stop laughing at him, Gold imagines, if only he can become Secretary of State. Heller's comic vision of Washington almost allows the impossible to happen. Gold is called to the White House by a college friend now working as an "unnamed source" on the president's staff. Gold is tempted with possibilities of high office, but all is vague in a young administration that elevates doubletalk to new depths. He might just as well have fallen down with Alice into a wonderland of Mad Hatters.

Heller's inspired wordplay, so often the source of comedy in *Catch-22*, informs much of the dialogue in the Washington scenes. Gold is welcomed to the White House by his college friend: "We all feel it would be a good idea to start using you here as quickly as possible if we decide we want to use you at all" (41). When he is assigned to a presidential commission, Gold receives the following advice: "Do whatever you want as long as you do whatever we want. We have no ideas, and they're pretty firm. Seize control. This administration will back you all the way until it has to" (171). Gold's friend always talks in this way, and it soon grows predictable and tiresome. The political satire only becomes more interesting when the vanity, greed, and evil of Henry Kissinger are introduced as obsessions in Gold's mind.

While a variety of possible cabinet posts are being discussed with Gold, he is warned that he might have to get a better wife. "Belle would be okay for Labor or Agriculture," he is told, "but not for Secretary of State or Defense" (103). At first, Gold is elated by the idea of a new wife, and he proposes without delay to Andrea Conover, the daughter of "a dying career diplomat with tons of money and the best connections." Visits to the Conover estate in the Virginia hunt country provide a few of the more bizarre scenes in the novel. Pugh Biddle Conover proves to be a maniacal bigot, even more outspoken than Gold's own mad father. Heller brings the comedy full circle by hinting that Conover, the raving anti-Semite, once almost married Gold's insane stepmother. "How I dreaded the day," Conover recalls, "that I would have to face my family with the news that the girl I had resolved to marry was Jewish" (341-342). Her family, however, rejected him.

Heller readily admits that some of his comic situations are hardly original. "For *Good as Gold* I intentionally read English comic writers—Austen, Dickens, Wodehouse, and Waugh. I was looking for certain kinds of 'literary clichés.'" The sudden mention of a far-fetched coincidence is typical of the comic technique Heller may have learned from the English tradition. The scenes of Washington life in *Good as Gold* are a mixture of farce and satire. When dramatic timing and coincidence are most important, the novel moves in the direction of farce. When the comedy exposes the vices of government service—ambition, greed, vanity, etc.—the novel becomes a full scale political satire. What rescues the novel from shallow farce is Heller's remarkable satire of Henry Kissinger's role as superman.

The reputation of Kissinger is exploited by Heller to bring together the themes of Jewish experience and political satire. Even before Gold agreed to write a book about "the Jewish experience," he had been clipping newspaper articles in preparation for a book about Henry Kissinger. The clippings are reproduced in *Good as Gold*, and thus Heller sets up the possibility of playing off his fiction against evidence from the historical record. Although many novelists of the 1970s have experimented with a mixture of fact and fantasy, Heller has enjoyed a unique advantage. It is an irony of history that Heller and Kissinger were both writing books at the same time about Henry Kissinger. And it is a further irony that Kissinger often becomes a villain in the pages of *Good as Gold* and a hero in the pages of his own *White House Years* on the basis of the same actions and statements.

Jealousy, rage, and hatred do not begin to describe the vindictive passion of Gold's feelings about Kissinger. He believes that Kissinger should be "recalled in history . . . as an odious *shlump* who made war gladly" (317). Gold plans to have his book about the former Secretary of State expose his "low stature and despicable achievements" (326). The book will be called "The Little Prussian" because in the secret heart of his jealous rage Gold is convinced that Kissinger is a closet Nazi and not a Jew at all.

During his service in Washington on a presidential commission, Gold has a comic opportunity to test his "covert and remarkable hypothesis that Henry Kissinger was not a Jew." Also serving on the commission is a nameless "silver-haired former governor of Texas with a chiseled cleft in his chin and a reputation for emanating authority" (172). This cartoon imitation of John Connally boasts about a showdown he once enjoyed with Kissinger: "And from that time on I knew I had his pecker in my pocket" (393). Gold cannot resist the question—"Was it circumcised?" The words spoken by the fictional Connally in the novel are actually a direct quote from his mentor, L. B. Johnson, at the time he was the majority leader of the U. S. Senate. Heller also uses the statement as one of the two epigraphs to the novel, thus adding another mirror to the reflections of history and fiction.

While the hero of Heller's novel is trying to test his theories about Kissinger, he is further outraged to hear that the former Secretary of State is busy writing his own history. There is no doubt in Gold's mind about who is better qualified—"Gold, who'd collected everything by and about Kissinger ever published, could certainly do a better job than Kissinger on a book about Kissinger." Gold is convinced that Kissinger will be "oblivious to the despicable character of his small actions and the bloody catastrophies resulting from his large ones." Gold does not question his own moral superiority as he plots to expose and disgrace his rival. "Let the shuttling little bastard publish first if he dared!" No expression of vindictive fury, however, is enough to ease the jealous pain that rises in Gold when he thinks of how much money Kissinger's book will make.

The irony of Heller's novel, of course, is that Gold has been tempted to follow in the very footsteps of the man he detests. He would like to prove that Kissinger is not a Jew because that would allow him to become the first Jewish Secretary of State. Gold's hatred is not only mixed with jealousy, his violent criticism of Kissinger is also a compound of insecurity and self-doubt. If his family and friends are often treating him as if he were a fool, it follows that Gold desperately wants to transfer that image to Kissinger. There is no way that Gold can win. His family will be impressed if he becomes Secretary of State, but Gold himself will know that he has only become the very figure that he has always despised.

The most dangerous father in the novel is not Julius Gold who "had always considered his son a *schmuck*," nor Pugh Conover who says: "It's not merely because you're jewish that I don't like you," but Henry Kissinger who acts out the role of superman that Gold is tempted to imitate. The hero of Heller's novel must demythologize the role of superman in order to free himself from its vain images of power. Only by mocking the career of Kissinger can Gold come to terms with his own ambition and his own limitations. This happens when Gold inveighs against the image of Kissinger with such bitter passion that his invective spills forth in abusive Yiddish. Only then is Gold willing to give up his expectations of high office, forget about his engagement to Conover's daughter, abandon the writing of his Kissinger book, and finally return to his own wife and family.

Gold has been able to purge himself of his worst aspirations by discovering at the height of his passion all of the Yiddish terms he needs to hurl against the object of his fury. Throughout the novel Gold has been uncomfortable with being a Jew. At the beginning he agrees to write about "the Jewish experience," but then he cannot decide how to start. While his book remains unwritten, he has the experience of testing the various father-figures: Julius Gold, Conover, and Kissinger. Each pretends to be a different kind of superman, and Gold must learn to unmask all of them. Julius is revealed as an "autocratic old four-flusher," Conover is exposed as a raving anti-Semite, and Kissinger as a hypocrite who "made war like a Nazi." Only when Gold can reject the authority represented by each potential father is he then capable of fully accepting himself. At that point he is also ready to accept being a Jew. The passionate flow of Yiddish is one indication that his own insecurity and self-doubt have finally been transcended.

The second epigraph to the novel is a quote from Bernard Malamud: "If you ever forget you're a Jew, a gentile will remind you." All of Gold's encounters in Washington are such reminders. His friend at the White House talks to Gold about "your kind," and advises him to finish his book on the Jewish experience "while there's still time." Conover calls him "Goldberg, Goldfarb, Finegold, Goldfedder, Goldenrod, Manishevitz, Schwartz," etc., etc. The silver-haired former governor of Texas also tells Gold that "a Jew always needs friends in Washington, because he doesn't really belong here." Gold especially hates himself for having to play the role of humble office seeker in front of all of these men: "How much lower would he crawl to rise to the top" (343)? The image of Henry Kissinger kneeling in prayer next to Richard Nixon is particularly offensive to Gold, and it represents the betrayal of integrity, faith, and dignity that Gold learns in the novel to reject. After he has stripped the mask of superman from the kneeling hypocrite, Gold is ready to accept himself.

There is another character in the book even worse than Kissinger in his willingness to kneel down with those who disdain his company. Harris Rosenblatt and Gold knew one another as students at Columbia. Rosenblatt now thinks well of himself as a financial counselor in Washington. The full extent of his self-betrayal is measured by the time he spends in the company of Pugh Biddle Conover. Rosenblatt makes frequent trips to the Conover estate in the hunt country of Virginia, where the demented old bigot tricks Rosenblatt into thinking that the sport of a country squire depends on how often he shoots his dogs. Rosenblatt, of course, does not understand that his fawning gullibility is the best sport. During a chance encounter of Gold and Rosenblatt in Washington, a few Yiddish words are slipped by Gold into the conversation:

> "I don't understand Yiddish," Harris Rosenblatt told
> Gold at once, "and any words I may have known as a child
> I have forgotten. Although," Harris Rosenblatt continued
> in a softer tone with a kind of confiding geniality, "I used to
> be Jewish, you know."
> "I used to be a hunchback."
> "Isn't it amazing," exclaimed Harris Rosenblatt in a
> glad cry, "how we've both been able to change!" (345)

Gold is constantly embarrassed by his own vain pursuit of high office, but he goes along with the game until the very night of the Embassy Ball where he expects finally to meet the President. Gold arrives at the Ball disguised in formal dress, but instead of meeting the President, he suddenly receives the news of his brother's death. Heller's sense of dramatic timing is pefect: "As Gold pulled away he saw the President's car arriving" (394). The death of his older brother will force Gold to finally assume responsibility for his own family. He leaves Washington immediately, thus leaving behind him the world of false supermen, pseudo fathers, and gentile Jews. Gold's return to his family in New York brings the novel full circle. Beyond the unmasking of false idols and the political satire of vanity in high places, Gold finally visits the cemetery to place a pebble on his mother's grave. Ready at last to make peace with his origins, he puts his arms around the headstone which is covered with Hebrew characters he cannot read. At the end of the novel he is finally ready to begin his book about "the Jewish experience."

Notes

[1] Gladwin Hill, "Newcomer Author of Remarkable War Novel," *Los Angeles Mirror*, 23 October 1961, Sec. 3, p. 1.

[2] W. J. Miller, *Joseph Heller's Catch-22* (New York: Monarch Press, 1971), p. 5.

[3] John Aldridge, "Vision of a Man Raging in a Vacuum," *Saturday Review World*, 19 October 1974, pp. 18-21.

[4] Paul Krassner, "An Impolite Interview with Joseph Heller," *The Realist*, 39 (November 1962), pp. 18-31.

[5] Jack Siegel, "Book Nook," *Baltimore Jewish Times*, 3 January 1975.

[6] Joseph Heller, *Good as Gold* (New York: Simon and Schuster, 1979), p. 13. All further references to this edition are cited parenthetically.

Postscript

The decade has become history. How many of its books will be remembered as literature? The authors in this study have continued to influence their critical standing by the publication of several new volumes of fiction and criticism. Despite all predictions about the death of the novel, it continues to be the dominant form of contemporary literature.

The shifting critical fashions of the decade apparently have not distracted writers from the power inherent in the roots of narrative form. How to retell an old story for a contemporary audience has been a challenge for many of the authors in this study. The examples of legend and drama are clearly alive in the imagination of Saul Bellow when he reshapes the dilemma of Lear into the contemporary plight of Mr. Sammler. The narrative forms of classical myth are evident in the mind of Margaret Atwood when she finds a way for her contemporary heroine to make a descent into the underworld. Whether it is the haunted territory of Poe reclaimed by John Hawkes, or the fantasy of Kafka redesigned by Philip Roth, the history of literature is a record of adaptation and renewal. The recent code word for this phenomenon is "intertextuality," but recognition of the process is as old as literary criticism. Contemporary interest in intertextuality, however, does extend beyond the familiar study of literary influences to investigate all discursive codes that make possible the meaning of literature.[1] The coherent tradition of narrative form is suggested by Yeats's symbol of history and culture—"the spreading laurel tree." The branches continue to flourish because their life is drawn from deep roots.

This famous symbol of organic form, however, may seem to be an anachronism for a period when some critics declare that fiction is supposed to be self-reflexive, discontinuous, inconclusive, self-contradictory, and perhaps even random.[2] Indeed, in a much quoted essay from the end of the 1960s, John Barth announced that the forms of narrative were nearly exhausted.[3] After a decade of ignoring his own predictions, however, Barth neatly reversed his critical posture in "The Literature of Replenishment."[4] Barth's debate with himself is typically full of spirit and wit, but the reversal of argument underscores its futility. If narrative forms are defined as projections of human nature, then fiction becomes an infinite process, and its forms can neither be exhausted nor replenished.

How narrative forms are related to human nature has been a major focus of criticism from the time of Aristotle, and all major theories of imitation and expression are attempts to solve this problem. The most famous definition of realism, however, comes from a fictional character. Hamlet distracts himself from the task of vengeance long enough to comment on the purpose of drama, which he says is "to hold . . . the mirror up to nature." Shakespeare no doubt wished his audience to believe in the "reality" of the dramatic illusion, but he also knew how the imagination brings forth "the forms of things unknown," and how the poet's pen "gives to airy nothing/A local habitation and a name." When the illusion does not call attention to itself as such, then the art may be seen as realistic. When the writer does remind us of his own narrative or dramatic strategy, perhaps by self-parody, discontinuity, exaggeration, or irony, then the contour of the mirror becomes at least as important as its content. Either practice must be as old as storytelling itself, and while several contemporary authors have stressed the ways of self-conscious experimentation, perhaps because of impatience with conventional forms, neither practice holds sway over contemporary literature. Indeed, half the novelists in this study—Bellow, Atwood, Morrison, Hawkes, and Roth—are working in forms of realism which draw their power from a wide range of discourse including drama, fiction, history, and classical myth.

The other half—Updike, Vonnegut, Doctorow, Vidal, and Heller—are also holding a mirror up to nature, but they do so in a way that calls more attention to the very process of art itself. Vonnegut thus appears as a character in his own fiction, and the self-parody reveals the different levels of illusion. Vidal and Heller use the trick of exaggeration—*Kalki* and *Good as Gold* are deliberately absurd, unreal, impossible—to project their religious and political satire. Updike adds a second mirror to his narrative by drawing fictional characters that are in turn reflected from the shadow history of the television screen. The TV coverage of Apollo 11 and Vietnam thus becomes an illusion of history for the background of *Rabbit Redux*. Perhaps the most daring experiment in the self-conscious play with mirror images comes in Doctorow's *Ragtime*, where a collage of history and fiction is reflected by the unseen narrator.

Experimentation with narrative form may generate its own critical interest, and receive some labels of questionable value such as "post-contemporary," but it does not mean that the forms of the novel are either exhausted or replenished.[5] There is finally no contradiction between describing the history of literature as a "spreading laurel tree" and a "house of mirrors." (The critical terms in vogue are "diachronic" and "synchronic.") Literature has always been both, and contemporary fiction is no exception. The storytellers in this study all reveal a double awareness of history and fiction in the 1970s—the result is the form and challenge of a remarkable decade of novels.

Notes

[1] See Jonathan Cullers, "Presupposition and Intertextuality," *The Pursuit of Signs: Semiotics, Literature, Deconstruction* (Ithaca, New York: Cornell University Press, 1981), pp. 100-118.

[2] See David Lodge, "Postmodernist Fiction," *The Modes of Modern Writing* (Ithaca, New York: Cornell University Press, 1977), pp. 220-245.

[3] John Barth, "The Literature of Exhaustion," *The Atlantic* (August 1967).

[4] John Barth, "The Literature of Replenishment: Postmodernist Fiction," *The Atlantic* (January 1980).

[5] The dubious credit for proclaiming "the death of Modernism and the birth pangs of Post-Modernism" belongs to Leslie Fielder. See "Cross the Border, Close the Gap," *Playboy* (December 1969). Reprinted in *The Collected Essays of Leslie Fielder* (New York: Stein and Day, 1971). Jerome Klinkowitz coined the ironic label—"Post-Contemporary." See Jerome Klinkowitz, *Literary Disruptions: The Making of a Post-Contemporary American Fiction* (Urbana: University of Illinois Press, 1975).